CAMBRIDGE LIBRARY COLLECTION

Books of enduring scholarly value

Religion

For centuries, scripture and theology were the focus of prodigious amounts of scholarship and publishing, dominated in the English-speaking world by the work of Protestant Christians. Enlightenment philosophy and science, anthropology, ethnology and the colonial experience all brought new perspectives, lively debates and heated controversies to the study of religion and its role in the world, many of which continue to this day. This series explores the editing and interpretation of religious texts, the history of religious ideas and institutions, and not least the encounter between religion and science.

The Ninth Bridgewater Treatise

Charles Babbage (1791-1871) was an English mathematician, philosopher and mechanical engineer who invented the concept of a programmable computer. From 1828 to 1839 he held the Lucasian Professorship of Mathematics at Cambridge, whose holders have also included Isaac Newton and Stephen Hawking. A proponent of Natural Religion, he published The Ninth Bridgewater Treatise in 1837 as his personal response to The Bridgewater Treatises, a series of books on theology and science that had recently been published with the support of a legacy from the Earl of Bridgewater. Disputing the claim that science disfavours religion, Babbage wrote "that there exists no such fatal collision between the words of Scripture and the facts of nature." He argues on the basis of reason and experience alone, drawing a parallel between his work on the calculating engine and God as a divine programmer of the universe. Eloquently written, and underpinned by mathematical arguments, The Ninth Bridgewater Treatise is a landmark work of natural theology.

Cambridge University Press has long been a pioneer in the reissuing of out-of-print titles from its own backlist, producing digital reprints of books that are still sought after by scholars and students but could not be reprinted economically using traditional technology. The Cambridge Library Collection extends this activity to a wider range of books which are still of importance to researchers and professionals, either for the source material they contain, or as landmarks in the history of their academic discipline.

Drawing from the world-renowned collections in the Cambridge University Library, and guided by the advice of experts in each subject area, Cambridge University Press is using state-of-the-art scanning machines in its own Printing House to capture the content of each book selected for inclusion. The files are processed to give a consistently clear, crisp image, and the books finished to the high quality standard for which the Press is recognised around the world. The latest print-on-demand technology ensures that the books will remain available indefinitely, and that orders for single or multiple copies can quickly be supplied.

The Cambridge Library Collection will bring back to life books of enduring scholarly value (including out-of-copyright works originally issued by other publishers) across a wide range of disciplines in the humanities and social sciences and in science and technology.

The Ninth Bridgewater Treatise

CHARLES BABBAGE

CAMBRIDGE
UNIVERSITY PRESS

CAMBRIDGE UNIVERSITY PRESS

Cambridge, New York, Melbourne, Madrid, Cape Town, Singapore,
São Paolo, Delhi, Dubai, Tokyo

Published in the United States of America by Cambridge University Press, New York

www.cambridge.org
Information on this title: www.cambridge.org/9781108000000

© in this compilation Cambridge University Press 2009

This edition first published 1837
This digitally printed version 2009

ISBN 978-1-108-00000-0 Paperback

THE NINTH

BRIDGEWATER TREATISE.

A FRAGMENT.

BY

CHARLES BABBAGE, ESQ.

" We may thus, with the greatest propriety, deny to the mechanical philosophers and mathematicians of recent times any authority with regard to their views of the administration of the universe; we have no reason whatever to expect from their speculations any help, when we ascend to the first cause and supreme ruler of the universe. But we might perhaps go farther, and assert that they are in some respects less likely than men employed in other pursuits, to make any clear advance towards such a subject of speculation."—*Bridgewater Treatise, by the* Rev. Wm. Whewell, p. 334.

LONDON:

JOHN MURRAY, ALBEMARLE STREET.

M DCCC XXXVII.

CONTENTS.

B

iv

CONTENTS.

PREFACE.

THE volume here presented to the public does
not form a part of that series of works composed at the desire of the trustees who directed
the application of the bequest of £8000, by
the late Earl of Bridgewater, for the purpose
of advancing arguments in favour of Natural
Religion.

I have, however, thought, that in furthering the intentions of the testator, by publishing some reflections on that subject, I might be permitted to connect with them a title which has now become familiarly associated, in the public mind, with the evidences in favour of Natural Religion.

The Bridgewater Treatises were restricted by the founder to the subject of Natural Religion; and I had intended not to have deviated from their example. In the single instance in which the question of miracles has been discussed, I was led so irresistibly, by the very nature of the illustrations employed in the former argument, to the view there proposed, that I trust to being excused for having ventured one step beyond the strict limits of that argument, by entering on the first connecting link between natural religion and revelation.

The same argument will produce very various

degrees of conviction on different minds; and much of this difference will depend on the extent of previous information, and on the strength of the reasoning faculty in those to whom the argument is addressed. To the great variety, therefore, of the illustrations which have been adduced in proof of design and of benevolence in the works of the Creator, there can be no objection. In truth, to the cultivated eye of science, the origin and consequences of the mightiest hurricane, as well as those of the smallest leaf it scatters in its course, equally lead to the inference of a designing power, the more irresistibly the more extensive the knowledge which is brought to bear on those phenomena.

One of the chief defects of the Treatises above referred to appears to me to arise from their not pursuing the argument to a sufficient extent. When a multitude of apparently unconnected facts is traced up to some

common principle, we feel spontaneously an
admiration for him who has explained to us
the connexion; and if, advancing another
stage in the investigation, he prove that other
facts, apparently at variance with that principle, are not merely no exceptions, but are
themselves inevitable consequences of its application, our admiration of the principle,
and our respect for its discoverer, are still
further enhanced.

But if this respect and admiration are
yielded to the mere interpreter of Nature's
laws, how much more exalted must those
sentiments become when applied to the Being
who called such principles into living existence by creating matter subservient to their
dominion—whose mind, intimately cognizant
of the remotest consequences of the present
as well as of all other laws, decreed existence
to that one alone, which should comprehend
within its grasp the completion of its destiny—

which should require no future intervention
to meet events unanticipated by its author, in
whose omniscient mind we can conceive no
infirmity of purpose—no change of intention!

The object of these pages, as of the Bridgewater Treatises, is to show that the power and
knowledge of the great Creator of matter and
of mind are unlimited. Deeply engaged in
those other pursuits from which my chief arguments are drawn, I regret the impossibility of
bestowing on their full development that time
and attention which the difficulty and importance of the subject equally deserve ; and in
committing these fragments to the press,
perhaps in too condensed a form, I wish them
to be considered merely as suggestions intended to direct the reader's attention to lines
of argument which appear to me new, and to
views of nature which appear more magnifi-
cent, than those with which I was previously
acquainted.

Probably I should not have been induced
to place my reflections on the subject before
the public, had I not, in common with other
cultivators of the more abstract branches of
mathematical science, felt that a prejudice,
which I had believed to have been long eradi-
cated from every cultivated mind, had lately
received support, at least to a certain extent,
from a chapter in the first* of the Bridgewater
Treatises; and in a still greater degree, from
a work of a far different order—one, however,
which derived its only claim to notice from the
circumstance of its appearing under the sanc-
tion of the University of Oxford.

The prejudice to which I allude is, *that the
pursuits of science are unfavourable to religion.*

There are two classes of men most deeply
impressed with the conviction of the very

* It was the first in the order of publication.

limited extent of human knowledge—those
whose contracted information renders them
eminent examples of the fact, and those whose
wide grasp of many of its profoundest branches
has taught them, by lengthened experience, that
each accession to their stock but enables them
to view a larger portion of its illimitable field.
Those who belong to the first of these classes
must acquire the alphabet of science, in order
to understand knowledge, and the elements
of modesty, to use it with dignity. When
they have thus graduated in the " infant
school" of philosophy, they may perhaps
understand the argument, and perchance be
worthy of a reply,—but not till then.

In that chapter of the first Bridgewater
Treatise to which I have referred, the charge
seems not even to be limited to those who
pursue that branch of science which is con-
versant with the properties of pure number,
and with abstractions of a like nature, but

applies to all who cultivate deductive processes
of reasoning.

It is maintained by the author, that long
application to such inquiries disqualifies the
mind from duly appreciating the force of that
kind of evidence which alone can be adduced
in favour of Natural Theology.

" We may thus, with the greatest propriety, deny to the
mechanical philosophers and mathematicians of recent times
any authority with regard to their views of the administration of the universe ; we have no reason whatever to expect
from their speculations any help, when we ascend to the
first cause and supreme ruler of the universe. But we
might perhaps go farther, and assert that they are in some
respects less likely than men employed in other pursuits,
to make any clear advance towards such a subject of speculation."—*Bridgewater Treatise, by the* Rev. Wm. Whewell,
p. 334.

Admitting, for the sake of argument, that
there have been individuals, possessed of high
intellectual powers, successfully devoted to
those subjects, who have arrived by reasoning
at conclusions respecting the First Cause,

totally opposite to those entertained by **Mr.**
Whewell and myself, **I** should still be very
reluctant to endeavour to invalidate the influence of their conclusions, by any inquiry
either into their intellectual or their moral
character. Reasoning is to be combated and
refuted by reasoning alone. Any endeavour to
raise a prejudice, or throw the shadow of an
imputation, either implies the existence of
some latent misgiving in the minds of those
who employ such weapons, or is a tacit admis-
sion that the question is beyond the grasp of
one at least of the debaters.

Who that has studied their works ever
dreamed of inquiring into the moral or intellectual character of Euclid or Archimedes, for
the purpose of confirming or invalidating his
belief in their conclusions? Who that possesses confidence in his own reason, justified
by a laborious cultivation and successful
exercise of that faculty, fails to anatomize and

refute the arguments, rather than analyze the mental or moral habits of those from whom he differs ?

The only case in which such extraneous matters can be fairly called in, is when facts are stated resting on testimony. Then it is not only just, but it is necessary for the sake of truth, to inquire into the habits of mind of him by whom they are adduced;— whether he possesses sufficient talent and precision to enable him to state precisely what his senses convey to him, and nothing more; or, if he receive information from others, whether he is credulous or cautious. In both cases, it is necessary to inquire into moral feelings, in order to be assured that there is no wilful mis-statement in the groundwork of his reasoning. And even when this is well established, it is still ne- cessary to inquire whether he had any personal, professional, or pecuniary interest

which may insensibly have influenced his
mind in one direction.

Such I conceive to be the sound distinction
between those branches of knowledge resting
on facts open to the observation of all, supported by reasoning addressed to the under-
standings of all, — and those other branches
in which reasoning is mixed up with testimony. In the former, the argument is every
thing—the character nothing: in the latter,
the character must be sifted as well as the
arguments.

Feeling convinced that the truths of Natural
Religion rest on foundations far stronger than
those of any human testimony; that they are
impressed in indelible characters, by almighty
power, on every fragment of the material
world, I cannot but regret that reflections
should have been made, in connexion with
this subject, calculated to throw the least

shadow of doubt on evidence otherwise irresistible.

As, however, these views of the nature of
the question may not bring that conviction
to other minds, which they do to my own,
and as *one* of the *disturbing forces* which act
on our minds has been strongly put forward,
it is but justice to state the whole of them.
It requires but little insight into man's
heart to perceive that profession and professional advancement — that power and
wealth — have a far more frequent and more
effective influence on his judgment than any
mental habits he may be supposed to have
cultivated.

It may be right then to state, that the
author of these pages has always been an ardent
but not an exclusive cultivator of some of
the more abstract branches of mathematical
science. In pursuing one of those inquiries,

amongst the most recondite and apparently
the most removed from any practical application, he was struck with the bearing of some
of the results which presented themselves, on
the question of Natural Religion; and these
he has endeavoured to place before the reader,
in the following pages.

The author belongs to no profession in
which he can hope for advancement, if he successfully advocate one side of the question, or
in which his prospects can be injured by can-
didly stating any arguments on the other.
He has not been invited by men high in the
State, and deservedly respected, to support
that great basis which precedes all revelation,
and on which it must all rest. Nor has any
sum of money been assigned to him, that,
whatever the mercantile success or failure
of the present volume may be, he shall,
on its publication, reap a large pecuniary
reward.

Having chosen a career to which the institutions of the country hold out none of those great prizes that stimulate professional exertions, and which constrain men to yield a certain degree of deference to the opinions, sound or unsound, of their countrymen, he has, on the one hand, nothing to hope from their approbation, and, on the other, is equally exempt from any fear of their censure ; and, had his conviction been as strongly opposed to the doctrines this Fragment advocates, as it is in their favour, he would, had a fit occasion presented itself, fearlessly have laid before the world the arguments which had forced his mind to that conviction.

In conclusion, I have to express to my fellow-labourers in the cause, my hope that they will put no unkind interpretation on these remarks, which, founded on principles of human nature, are necessarily of general application ; that they will see that motives alien, in my own opinion, to the subject, having been once introduced, candour to those who differ from us, as well as a deference to truth itself, compelled me to state them fully.

CHARLES BABBAGE.

DORSET-STREET,
MANCHESTER-SQUARE,
April 1837.

c 2

The following account of the origin of the Bridgewater Treatises, is extracted from one of these
works:—

" The Right Honourable and Reverend Francis Henry, Earl of
Bridgewater, died in the month of February, 1829; and, by his
last will and testament, bearing date the 25th of February, 1825,
he directed certain Trustees therein named, to invest in the public
funds the sum of eight thousand pounds sterling; this sum, with
the accruing dividends thereon, to be held at the disposal of
the President, for the time being, of the Royal Society of London,
to be paid to the person or persons nominated by him. The testator further directed, that the person or persons selected by the
said President should be appointed to write, print, and publish,
one thousand copies of a work "On the Power, Wisdom, and
Goodness of God, as manifested in the Creation;" illustrating such
work by all reasonable arguments, as, for instance, the variety
and formation of God's creatures in the animal, vegetable, and
mineral kingdoms; the effect of digestion, and thereby of conversion; the construction of the hand of man, and an infinite variety
of other arguments: as also by discoveries, ancient and modern,
in arts, sciences, and the whole extent of literature. He desired,
moreover, that the profits arising from the sale of the works
so published should be paid to the authors of the works.

The late President of the Royal Society, Davies Gilbert, Esq.,
requested the assistance of his Grace the Archbishop of Canterbury,
and of the Bishop of London, in determining upon the best mode
of carrying into effect the intentions of the testator. Acting with
their advice, and with the concurrence of a nobleman immediately
connected with the deceased, Mr. Davies Gilbert appointed eight
gentlemen to write separate Treatises on the different branches of
the subject."

Of the eight gentlemen so appointed, four were of the clerical, and four of the medical, profession. Their names, and the subjects assigned to them, are as follows:—

1. The Rev. Thomas Chalmers, D.D., Professor of Divinity in the University of Edinburgh—" On the Adaptation of External Nature to the Moral and Intellectual Constitution of Man."

2. The Rev. Wm. Buckland, D.D., F.R.S., Canon of Christ Church, and Professor of Geology in the University of Oxford—" On Geology and Mineralogy."

3. The Rev. Wm. Whewell, M.A., F.R.S., Fellow of Trinity College, Cambridge—" On Astronomy and General Physics."

4. The Rev. Wm. Kirby, M.A., F.R.S.—" On the History, Habits, and Instincts of Animals."

5. John Kidd, M.D., F.R.S., Regius Professor of Medicine in the University of Oxford—" On the Adaptation of External Nature to the Physical Condition of Man."

6. Sir Charles Bell, K.H., F.R.S.—" The Hand: its Mechanism and Vital Endowments, as evincing Design."

7. Peter Mark Roget, M.D., Fellow of, and Secretary to, the Royal Society—" On Animal and Vegetable Physiology."

8. Wm. Prout, M.D., F.R.S.—" On Chemistry, Meteorology, and the Function of Digestion."

CHAP. I.

NATURE OF THE ARGUMENT.

THE notions we acquire of contrivance and design arise from comparing our observations on the works of other beings with the intentions of which we are conscious in our own undertakings. We take the highest and best of human faculties, and, exalting them in our imagination to an unlimited extent, endeavour to attain an imperfect conception of that Infinite Power which created every thing around us. In pursuing this course, it is evident that we are liable to impress upon the notion of Deity thus shadowed out, many traces of those imperfections in our own limited faculties which are best known to those who have most deeply cultivated them. It is also evident that all those discoveries which arm human reason with new power, and all additions to our acquaintance with the material world, must from time to time render a revision of that notion necessary. The present seems to be a fit occasion for such a revision.

Many excellent and religious persons not deeply versed in what they mistakenly call "*human knowledge*," but which is in truth the interpretation of those laws that God himself has impressed on his creation, have endeavoured to discover proofs of design in a multitude of apparent adaptations of means to ends, and have represented the Deity as perpetually interfering, to alter for a time the laws he had previously ordained; thus by implication denying to him the possession of that foresight which is the highest attribute of omnipotence. Minds of this order, insensible of the existence of that combining and generalising faculty which gives to human intellect its greatest development, and tied down by the trammels of their own peculiar pursuits, have in their mistaken zeal not perceived their own unfitness for the mighty task, and have ventured to represent the Creator of the universe as fettered by the same infirmities as those by which their own limited faculties are subjugated. To causes of this kind must in some measure be attributed an opinion which has been industriously spread, that minds highly imbued with mathematical knowledge are disqualified, by the possession of that knowledge, and by the habits of mind produced during its acquisition, from rightly appreciating the works of the Creator.

At periods and in countries in which the knowledge of the priests exceeded that of the people, science has always been held up by the

former class as an object of regard, and its
crafty possessors have too frequently defiled its
purity by employing their knowledge for the
delusion of the people.   On the other hand,
at times and in countries in which the knowledge of the people has advanced beyond
that of the priesthood, the ministers of the
temple have too often been afraid of the
advance of knowledge, and have threatened
with the displeasure of the Almighty those
engaged in employing the faculties he has
bestowed on the study of the works he has
created.   At the present period, when knowledge is so universally spread that neither
class is far in advance of the other,—when
every subject is submitted to unbounded
discussion,—when it is at length fully acknow-
ledged that truth alone can stand unshaken by
perennial attacks, and that error, though for
centuries triumphant, must fall at last, and
leave behind no ashes from which it may
revive, the authority of names has but little
weight: facts and arguments are the basis of

creeds, and convictions so arrived at are the more deeply seated, and the more enduring, because they are not the wild fancies of passion or of impulse, but the deliberate results of reason and reflection.

It is a condition of our race that we must ever wade through error in our advance towards truth ; and it may even be said that in many cases we exhaust almost every variety of error before we attain the desired goal. But truths, once reached by such a course, are always most highly valued ; and when, in addition to this, they have been exposed to every variety of attack which splendid talents quickened into energy by the keen perception of personal interests can suggest,—when they have revived undying from unmerited neglect; when the anathema of spiritual, and the arm of secular power have been found as impotent in suppressing, as their arguments were in refuting them, then they are indeed irresistible. Thus tried and thus triumphant in

the fiercest warfare of intellectual strife, even
the temporary interests and furious passions
which urged on the contest, have contributed
in no small measure to establish their value,
and thus to render these truths the permanent
heritage of our race.

Viewed in this light, the propagation of an
error, although it may be unfavourable or
fatal to the temporary interest of an individual,
can never be long injurious to the cause of
truth. It may, at a particular time, retard its
progress for a while, but it repays the transitory injury by a benefit as permanent as the
duration of the truth to which it was opposed.
This reasoning is offered for the purpose of
proving that the toleration of the fullest discussion is most advantageous to truth. It is
not offered as the advocate of or the apology
for error; and whilst it is admitted that every
person who wilfully puts forward as valid an
argument the soundness of which he doubts,
incurs a deep responsibility, it is also some

satisfaction to reflect that the delay thus occasioned to the great cause can be but small, and that those who in sincerity of heart maintain arguments which a more advanced state of knowledge shall prove to be erroneous, may yet ultimately contribute, by that very publication, to its speedier establishment.

CHAP. II.

THE estimate we form of the intellectual capacity of our race, is founded on an examination of those productions which have resulted from the loftiest flights of individual genius, or from the accumulated labours of generations of men, by whose long-continued exertions a body of science has been raised up, surpassing in its extent the creative powers of any individual, and demanding for its development a length of time, to which no single life extends.

The estimate we form of the Creator of the visible world rests ultimately on the same foundation. Conscious that we each of us employ, in our own productions, *means* intended to accomplish the objects at which we aim, and tracing throughout the actions and inventions of our fellow-creatures the same intention,— judging also, of their capacity by the fit selection they make of the means by which they work, we are irresistibly led, when we contemplate the natural world, to attempt to trace each existing fact presented to our senses to some precontrived arrangement, itself perhaps the consequence of a yet more general law; and where the most powerful aids by which we can assist our limited faculties fail in enabling us to detect such connexions, we still, and not the less, believe that a more extended inquiry, or higher powers, would enable us to discover them.

The larger the number of consequences resulting from any law, and the more they are foreseen, the greater the knowledge and intelligence we ascribe to the being by which it was ordained. In the earlier stages of our knowledge, we behold a multitude of distinct laws, all harmonizing to produce results which we deem beneficial to our own species: as science advances, many of these minor laws merge into some more general principles; and with its higher progress these secondary principles appear, in their turn, the mere consequences of some still more general law. Such has been the case in two of the most curious and most elaborately cultivated branches of human knowledge, the sciences of astronomy and optics. All analogy leads us to infer, and new discoveries continually direct our expectation to the idea, that the most extensive laws to which we have hitherto attained, converge to some few simple and general principles, by which the whole of the material universe is sustained, and from which its infinitely varied phenomena emerge as the necessary consequences.*

* See Note A in the Appendix.

To illustrate the distinction between a system to which the restoring hand of its contriver is applied, either frequently or at distant intervals, and one which had received at its first formation the impress of the will of its author, foreseeing the varied but yet necessary laws of its action, throughout the whole extent of its existence, we must have recourse to some machine, the produce of human skill. But far as all such engines must ever be placed at an immeasurable interval below the simplest of Nature's works, yet, from the vastness of those cycles which even human contrivance in some cases unfolds to our view, we may perhaps be enabled to form a faint estimate of the magnitude of that lowest step in the chain of reasoning, which leads us up to Nature's God.

The illustration which I shall here employ will be derived from the results afforded by the Calculating Engine;* and this I am the

---

* The reader will find a short account of this engine in the Appendix, Note B.

D

more disposed to use, because my own views respecting the extent of the laws of Nature were greatly enlarged by considering it, and also because it incidentally presents matter for reflection on the subject of inductive reasoning. Nor will any difficulty arise from the complexity of that engine; no knowledge of its mechanism, nor any acquaintance with mathematical science, being necessary for comprehending the illustration, it being sufficient merely to conceive that computations of great complexity can be effected by mechanical means.

Let the reader imagine that such an engine has been adjusted; and that it is moved by a weight; and that he sits down before it, and observes a wheel, which revolves through a small angle round its axis, at short intervals, presenting to his eye, successively, a series of numbers engraved on its divided circumference.

Let the figures thus seen be the series 1, 2, 3, 4, 5, &c., of natural numbers, each of which exceeds its immediate antecedent by unity.

Now, reader, let me ask how long you will have counted before you are firmly convinced that the engine has been so adjusted that it will continue whilst its motion is maintained, to produce the same series of natural numbers? Some minds are so constituted, that after passing the first hundred terms, they will be satisfied that they are acquainted with the law. After seeing five hundred terms, few will doubt; and after the fifty-thousandth term the propensity to believe that the succeeding term will be fifty thousand and one, will be almost irresistible. That term *will* be fifty thousand and one; and the same regular succession will continue; the five-millionth and the fifty-millionth term will still appear in their expected order; and one unbroken chain of natural numbers will pass before your eyes, from *one* up to *one hundred million.*

True to the vast induction which has been made, the next succeeding term will be one hundred million and one; but the next number presented by the rim of the wheel, instead of being one hundred million and two, is one hundred million *ten thousand* and two. The whole series from the commencement being thus :—

$$
\begin{array}{l}
1 \\
2 \\
3 \\
4 \\
5 \\
\cdot\ \cdot\ \cdot \\
\cdot\ \cdot\ \cdot \\
\cdot\ \cdot\ \cdot\ \cdot\ \cdot \\
\cdot\ \cdot\ \cdot\ \cdot\ \cdot
\end{array}
$$

99,999,999
100,000,000
regularly as far as 100,000,001
100,010,002 the law changes
100,030,003
100,060,004
100,100,005
100,150,006
100,210,007
100,280,008

. . . .
. . . .

The law which *seemed* at first to govern this
series fails at the hundred million and second
term. This term is larger than we expected,
by 10,000. The next term is larger than was
anticipated, by 30,000, and the excess of each
term above what we had expected forms the
following table :—

10,000
30,000
60,000
100,000
150,000
::: :::

being, in fact, the series of *triangular numbers,* each multiplied by 10,000.

* The numbers 1, 3, 6, 10, 15, 21, 28, &c. are formed
by adding the successive terms of the series of natural
numbers thus ;

$$1 = 1.$$
$$1 + 2 = 3.$$
$$1 + 2 + 3 = 6.$$
$$1 + 2 + 3 + 4 = 10, \&c.$$

They are called triangular numbers, because a number
of points corresponding to any term can always be placed
in the form of a triangle, for instance :—

1   3   6   10

If we now continue to observe the numbers presented by the wheel, we shall find,
that for a hundred, or even for a thousand
terms, they continue to follow the new law
relating to the triangular numbers; but after
watching them for 2761 terms, we find that
this law fails in the case of the 2762d term.

If we continue to observe, we shall discover
another law then coming into action, which
also is dependent, but in a different manner,
on triangular numbers. This will continue
through about 1430 terms, when a new law is
again introduced, which extends over about
950 terms; and this too, like all its predecessors, fails, and gives place to other laws,
which appear at different intervals.

Now it must be remarked, that the law
*that each number presented by the Engine is
greater by unity than the preceding number,*
which law the observer had deduced from *an
induction of a hundred million instances,* was

not the true law that regulated its action ; and that the occurrence of the number 100,010,002 at the 100,000,002d term, was *as necessary a consequence* of the original adjustment, and might have been as fully foreknown at the commencement, as was the regular succession of any one of the intermediate numbers to its immediate antecedent. The same remark applies to the next *apparent* deviation from the new law, which was founded on an induction of 2761 terms, and also to the succeeding law; with this limitation only—that whilst their consecutive introduction at various definite intervals is a necessary consequence of the mechanical structure of the engine, our knowledge of analysis does not enable us to predict the periods themselves at which the more distant laws will be introduced.

Such are the facts which, by a certain adjustment of the Calculating Engine, would be presented to the observer. Now, let him imagine another engine, offering to him precisely

the same figures in the same order of succession; but let it be necessary for the maker
of that other engine, previously to each apparent change in the law, to make some new
adjustment in the structure of the engine itself,
in order to accomplish the ends proposed.
The first engine must be susceptible of having
embodied in its mechanical structure, that
more general law of which all the observed
laws were but isolated portions,—a law so
complicated, that analysis itself, in its present
state, can scarcely grasp the whole question.
The second engine might be of far simpler
contrivance; it must be capable of receiving
the laws impressed upon it from without, but
is incapable, by its own intrinsic structure, of
changing, at definite periods, and in unlimited
succession, those laws' by which it acts.
Which of these two engines would, in the
reader's opinion, give the higher proof of skill
in the contriver? He cannot for a moment
hesitate in pronouncing that that on which,
after its original adjustment, no superintend-

ance was required, displayed far greater in-
genuity than that which demanded, at every
change in its law, the intervention of its
contriver.

The engine we have been considering is but
a very small portion (about fifteen figures)
of a much larger one, which was preparing,
and partly executed; it was intended, when
completed, that it should have presented at
once to the eye about one hundred and thirty
figures. In that more extended form which
recent simplifications have enabled me to give
to machinery constructed for the purpose of
making calculations, it will be possible, by certain adjustments, to set the engine so that it
shall produce the series of natural numbers in
regular order, from unity up to a number expressed by more than a thousand places of
figures. At the end of that term, another and a
different law shall regulate the succeeding
terms; this law shall continue in operation perhaps for a number of terms, expressed by unity,

followed by a thousand zeros, or 10^{1000}; at which period another law shall be introduced, and, like its predecessors, govern the figures produced by the engine during a third of those enormous periods. This change of laws might continue without limit; each individual law destined to govern for millions of ages the calculations of the engine, and then give way to its successor to pursue a like career.*

Thus a series of laws, each simple in itself, successively spring into existence, at distances almost too great for human conception. The full expression of that wider law, which comprehends within it this unlimited sequence of minor consequences, may indeed be beyond the utmost reach of mathematical analysis: but of one remarkable fact, however, we are

* It has been supposed that ten turns of the handle of the calculating engine might be made in a minute, or about five hundred and twenty-six millions in a century. As in this case, each turn would make a calculation, after the lapse of a million of centuries, only the fifteenth place of figures would have been reached.

certain — that the mechanism brought into action for the purpose of changing the nature of the calculation from the production of its more elementary operations into those highly complicated ones of which we speak, is itself of the simplest kind.

In contemplating the operations of laws so uniform during such immense periods, and then changing so completely their apparent nature, whilst the alterations are in fact only the *necessary* consequences of some far higher law, we can scarcely avoid remarking the analogy which they bear to several of the phenomena of nature.

The laws of animal life which regulate the caterpillar, seem totally distinct from those which, in the subsequent stage of its existence, govern the butterfly. The difference is still more remarkable in the transformations undergone by that class of animals which spend the first portion of their life beneath the surface of the waters, and the latter part as inhabitants of air. It is true that the periods during which these laws exist are not, to our senses, enormous, like the mechanical ones above mentioned; but it cannot be doubted that, immeasurably more complex as they are, they were equally foreknown by their Author: and that the first creation of the egg of the moth, or the libellula, involved within its contrivance, as a necessary consequence, the whole of the subsequent transformations of every individual of their respective races.

In turning our views from these simple consequences of the juxtaposition of a few wheels, it is impossible not to perceive the parallel reasoning, as applied to the mighty and far more complex phenomena of nature. To call into existence all the variety of vegetable forms, as they become fitted to exist, by the successive adaptations of their parent earth, is undoubtedly a high exertion of creative power. When a rich vegetation has covered the globe, to create animals adapted to that clothing,

which, deriving nourishment from its luxuri-
ance, shall gladden the face of nature, is not
only a high but a benevolent exertion of
creative power. To change, from time to time,
after lengthened periods, the races which exist,
as altered physical circumstances may render
their abode more or less congenial to their
habits, by allowing the natural extinction of
some races, and by a new creation of others
more fitted to supply the place previously
abandoned, is still but the exercise of the same
benevolent power. To cause an alteration in
those physical circumstances—to add to the
comforts of the newly created animals — all
these acts imply power of the same order, a
perpetual and benevolent superintendence, to
take advantage of altered circumstances, for the
purpose of producing additional happiness.

But, to have *foreseen*, at the creation of
matter and of mind, that a period would arrive when matter, assuming its prearranged
combinations, would become susceptible of

the support of vegetable forms; that these
should in due time themselves supply
the pabulum of animal existence; that successive races of giant forms or of micro-
scopic beings should at appointed periods
necessarily rise into existence, and as inevitably yield to decay; and that decay and
death—the lot of each individual existence
—should also act with equal power on the
races which they constitute; that the extinction of every race should be as certain as the
death of each individual; and the advent of
new genera be as inevitable as the destruction of their predecessors;—to have foreseen
all these changes, and to have provided, by
one comprehensive law, for all that should
ever occur, either to the races themselves, to
the individuals of which they are composed,
or to the globe which they inhabit, manifests
a degree of power and of knowledge of a far
higher order.

The vast cycles in the geological changes

that have taken place in the earth's surface, of which we have ample evidence, offer another analogy in nature to those mechanical changes of law from which we have endeavoured to extract a *unit* sufficiently large to serve as an imperfect measure for some of the simplest works of the Creator.

The gradual advance of Geology, during the last twenty years, to the dignity of a science, has arisen from the laborious and extensive collection of facts, and from the enlightened spirit in which the inductions founded on those facts have been deduced and discussed. To those who are unacquainted with this science, or indeed to any person not deeply versed in the history of this and kindred subjects, it is impossible to convey a just impression of the nature of that evidence by which a multitude of its conclusions are supported :—evidence in many cases so irresistible, that the records of the past ages, to which it refers, are traced in language more imperishable than that of

the historian of any human transactions; the
relics of those beings, entombed in the strata
which myriads of centuries have heaped upon
their graves, giving a present evidence of their
past existence, with which no human testimony can compete. It is found that each
additional step, in the grouping together of
the facts of geology, confirms the view that
the changes of our planet, since it has been
the abode of man, is but as a page in the
massive volumes of its history, every leaf of
which, written in the same character, conveys
to the decypherer the idea of a succession
of the same causes acting with varying intensity, through unequal but enormous periods,
each period apparently distinguished by the
coming in or going out of new subsidiary laws,
yet all submitted to some still higher condition, which has stamped the mark of unity
on the series, and points to the conclusion
that the minutest changes, as well as those
transitions apparently the most abrupt, have
throughout all time been the necessary, the

inevitable consequences of some more comprehensive law impressed on matter at the dawn of its existence.

CHAP. III.

ARGUMENT TO SHOW THAT THE DOCTRINES IN
THE PRECEDING CHAPTER DO NOT LEAD TO
FATALISM.

IF all the combinations and modifications
of matter can be supposed to be traced up to
one general and comprehensive law, from
which every visible form, both in the organic
and inorganic world flows, as the necessary
consequence of the first impression of that
law upon matter, it might seem to follow that
Fate or Necessity governs all things, and that
the world around us may not be the result of
a contriving mind working for a benevolent
purpose.

Such, possibly, may be the first impression of this view of the subject; but it is an erroneous view,—one of those, perhaps, through which it is necessary to pass, in order to arrive at truth. Let us briefly review the labour which the human race has expended, in attaining the limited knowledge we possess. For about six thousand years man has claimed the earth as his heritage, and asserted his dominion over all other beings endued with life; yet, during a large portion of that period, how comparatively small has been his mental improvement! Until the invention of printing, the mass of mankind were in many respects almost the creatures of instinct. It is true, the knowledge possessed by each generation, instead of being the gift of Nature, was derived from the instruction of their predecessors; but, how little were those lessons improved by repeated communication! Transmitted most frequently by unenlightened instructors, they might lose, but could rarely gain in value.

Before the invention of printing, accidental position determined the opinions and the knowledge of the great mass of mankind. Oral information being almost the only kind accessible, each man shared the opinions of his kindred and neighbours ; and truth, which is ever most quickly and most surely elicited by discussion, lost all those advantages which diversity of opinion always produces for it. The minds of individual men, however powerful, could address themselves only to a very small portion of their fellow men ; their influence was restricted by space and limited by time, and their highest powers were not stimulated into action by the knowledge that their reasonings could have effect where their voices were unheard, or by the conviction that the truths they arrived at, and the discoveries they made, would extend beyond their country, and survive their age.

But, since the invention of printing, how different has been the position of mankind !

the nature of the instruction no longer depends entirely on the knowledge of the
instructor. The village school-master communicates to his pupils the power of using
an instrument by which not merely the best
of their living countrymen, but the greatest
and wisest men of all countries and all times,
may become their instructors. Even the elementary writings through which this art is
taught, give to the pupil, not the sentiments of
the teacher, but those which the public opinion
of his countrymen esteems most fit for the be-
ginner in knowledge. Thus the united opinions
of multitudes of human minds are brought
to bear even upon seemingly unimportant
points.

If such is the effect of the invention of
printing upon ordinary minds, its influence
over those more highly endowed is far greater.
To them the discussion of the conflicting opinions of different countries and distant ages,
and the establishment of new truths, presents

a field of boundless and exalted ambition.
Advancing beyond the knowledge of their
neighbours and countrymen, they may be exposed to those prejudices which result from
opinions long stationary ; but encouraged by
the approbation of the greatest of other nations, and the more enlightened of their own,—
knowing that time alone is wanting to complete
the triumph of truth, they may accelerate the
approaching dawn of that day which shall
pour a flood of light over the darkened intel-
lects of their thankless countrymen—content
themselves to exchange the hatred they experience from the honest and the dishonest into-
lerance of their contemporaries, for that higher
homage, alike independent of space and of time,
which their memory will for ever receive
from the good and the gifted of all countries
and all ages.

Until printing was very generally spread,
civilisation scarcely advanced by slow and lan-
guid steps; since this art has become cheap,

its advances have been unparalleled, and its rate of progress vastly accelerated.

It has been stated by some, that the civilisation of the Western World has resulted from its being the seat of the Christian religion : however much the mild tenor of its doctrines is calculated to assist in producing such an effect, that religion cannot but be injured by an unfounded statement. It is to the easy and cheap methods of communicating thought from man to man, which enable a country to sift, as it were, its whole people, and to produce, in its science, its literature, and its arts, not the brightest efforts of a limited class, but the highest exertions of the most powerful minds among a whole community ;—it is this which has given birth to the wide-spreading civilisation of the present day, and which promises a futurity yet more prolific. Whoever is acquainted with the present state of science and the mechanical arts, and looks back over the inventions and civilisation which the fourteen

centuries subsequent to the introduction of
Christianity have produced, and compares
them with the advances made during the succeeding four centuries following the invention
of printing, will have no doubt as to the effective cause.

It is during these last three or four centuries, that man, considered as a species, has
commenced the development of his intellectual faculties—that he has emerged from a position in which he was almost the creature of
instinct, to a state in which every step in advance facilitates the progress of his successors. In the first period, arts were discovered
by individuals, and lost to the race ; in the
latter, the diffusion of ideas enabled the reasoning of one class to unite with the observations of another, and the most advanced point
of one generation became the starting post
of the next.

It is during this portion of our history that

man has become acquainted with his real position in the universe—that he has measured the distance from that which is to us the great fountain of light and heat—that he has traced the orbits of earth's sister spheres, and calculated the paths of all their dependent worlds—that he has arrived at the knowledge of a law—that of gravity, which appears to govern all matter, and whose remotest consequences, if first traced by his telescope, are found written in his theory; or, if first predicted by his theory, are verified by his observations.

Simple as that law now appears, and beautifully in accordance with all the observations of past and of present times, consider what it has cost of intellectual study. Copernicus, Galileo, Kepler, Euler, Lagrange, Laplace, all the great names which have exalted the character of man, by carrying out trains of reasoning unparalleled in every other science; these, and a host of others, each of whom might have been the Newton of another field, have all laboured to work out, the consequences which resulted from that single law which he discovered. All that the human mind has produced—the brightest in genius, or the most continuous in application, has been lavished on the details of the law of gravity.

Had that law been other than it is—had it been the inverse cube of the distance, for example, it would still have required an equal expense of genius and of perseverance to have worked out its details. But, between the laws represented by the inverse square, and the inverse cube of the distance, there are interposed an infinite number of other laws, each of which might have been the basis of a system requiring the most extensive knowledge to trace out its consequences. Between every law which can be expressed by whole numbers, whether it be direct or inverse, an infinity of others can still be interposed. All these might be again combined by two,

by three, or by any other combinations, and
new systems might be imagined,* submitted
to such laws. Thus, another infinity of laws,
of a far higher order—in fact, of an *infinitely*
higher order—might again be added to the list.
And this might still be increased by every other
combination, of which such laws admit, besides
that by addition, to which we have already
alluded, thus forming an infinity itself of so
high an order, that it is difficult to conceive.
Man has, as yet, no proof of the impossibility
of the existence of any of these laws. Each
might, for any reason we can assign, be the
basis of a creation different from our own.

It is at this point that skill and knowledge
re-enter the argument, and banish for ever the
dominion of chance. The Being who called

---

* Even beyond this, every law so imagined might be
interrupted by any discontinuous function ; and thus be
made to agree, for any period, with laws of simpler form,
and yet deviate, in one single, or in a certain limited number of cases, and then agree with it for ever.

into existence this creation, of which we are parts, must have chosen the present form, the present laws, in preference to the infinitely infinite variety which he might have willed into existence. He must have known and fore- seen all, even the remotest consequences of every one of those laws, to have penetrated but a little way into one of which has ex- hausted the intellect of our whole species.

But, if such is the view we must take of the knowledge of the Creator, when contemplating the laws of inanimate matter—laws into whose consequences it has cost us such accumulated labour to penetrate—what language can we speak, when we consider that the laws which connect matter with animal life may be as in- finitely varied as those which regulate material existence? The little we know, might, per- haps, lead us to infer a far more unlimited field of choice. The chemist has reduced all the materials of the earth with which we are acquainted, to about fifty simple bodies;

but the zoologist can make no such reductions in his science. He must claim for one scarcely noticed class — that of intestinal parasites — about thirty thousand species; and, not to mention the larger classes of animals, who shall number the species of infusoria in living waters, still less those which are extinct, and whose scarcely visible relics are contained within the earth, in almost mountain masses.*

In absolute ignorance of any — even the smallest link of those chains which bind life to matter, or that still more miraculous one, which connects mind to both, we can only pursue our path by the feeble light of analogy, and humbly hope that the Being, whose power

---

* Professor Ehrenberg, of Berlin, has discovered that the tripoli employed in that city for polishing metals, which is dug up at Bilin, in Bohemia, consists almost entirely of the siliceous remains of infusoria, of a species so minute, that about 41,000 millions of them weigh 220 grains, and occupy the space of a cubic inch. The reader will find a translation of the highly interesting papers of Professor Ehrenberg, in the third number of the " Scientific Memoirs," published by Mr. R. Taylor.

and benevolence are unbounded, may enable us, in some further stage of our existence, to read another page in the history of his mighty works.

Enough, however, and more than enough, may be gathered even from our imperfect acquaintance with matter, and some few of its laws, to prove the unbounded knowledge which must have preceded their organization.

CHAP. IV.

ON THE ACCOUNT OF THE CREATION, IN THE FIRST CHAPTER OF GENESIS.

A STRANGE and singular argument has frequently been brought against the truth of the facts presented to us by Geology,—facts which every instructed person may confirm by the evidence of his senses. It has been stated that they cannot be true; because, if admitted, they lead inevitably to the conclusion, that the earth has existed for an enormous period, extending, perhaps, over millions of years; whereas, it was supposed, from the history of the creation as delivered by Moses, that the earth was first created about six thousand years ago.

A different interpretation has been lately put upon that passage of the sacred writings ; and, according to the highest authorities of the present time, it was not the intention of the writer of the book of Genesis to assign this date to the creation of our globe, but only to that of its most favoured inhabitants.

Now, it is obvious that additional observations, and another advance in science, may at no distant period render necessary another interpretation of the Mosaic narrative ; and this again, at a more remote time, may be superseded by one more in accordance with the existing knowledge of that day. And thus, the authority of Scripture will be gradually undermined by the weak though well-intentioned efforts of its friends in its support. For it is clear that when a work, translated by persons most highly instructed in its language, and seeking, in plainness and sincerity, to understand its true meaning, admits of such discordant interpretations, it can have little authority as a history of the past, or a guide to the future.

It is time, therefore, to examine this question by another light, and to point out to those who support what is called the literal interpretation of Scripture, the precipice to which their doctrines, if true, would inevitably lead; and to show, not by the glimmerings of elaborate criticism, but by the plainest principles of common sense, that there exists no such fatal collision between the words of Scripture and the facts of nature.

And first, let us examine what must of necessity be the conclusion of any candid mind from the mass of evidence presented to it. Looking solely at the facts in which all capable of investigation agree—facts which it is needless to recite, they having been so fully and ably stated in the works of Mr. Lyell and

F

Dr. Buckland,—we there see, and with no theoretic eye, the remains of animated beings, more and more differing from existing races, as we descend in the series of strata. Not merely are the petrified bones preserved, displaying marks of the insertion of every muscle necessary for the movement of the living animal, but in some cases we discover even the secretions of their organs, prepared either for nourishment or for defence. Almost every stratum we pause to examine, affords indubitable evidence of having, at some former period, existed for ages at the bottom of some lake or estuary, some inland sea, or some extensive ocean teeming with animal existence, or of having been the surface of a country covered with vegetation, which perished and was renewed at distant and successive periods.

Those, however, who, without the knowledge which enables them to form an opinion on the subject, feel any latent wish that this evidence should be overthrown, would do well to remember that geology also furnishes strong evidence in favour of the much more direct statement of Moses, as to the recent creation of man. And although we must ever feel a certain degree of caution in admitting negative evidence as conclusive; yet, in the present instance, the multitude of fossil bones which have been discovered, and which, when examined by persons *duly qualified* for the task, have been uniformly pronounced to be those of various tribes of animals, and not those of the human race, undoubtedly affords strong corroborative evidence in confirmation of the Mosaic account.

In truth, the mass of evidence which combines to prove the great antiquity of the earth, is so irresistible, and so unshaken by any opposing facts, that none but those who are alike incapable of observing the facts and of appreciating the reasoning, can for a moment conceive the present state of its surface to have been the result of only six thousand years of existence.

What, then, have those accomplished who have restricted the Mosaic account of creation to that diminutive period, which is, as it were, but a span in the duration of the earth's existence, and who have imprudently rejected the testimony of the senses, when opposed to their philological criticisms? Undoubtedly, if they have succeeded in convincing either themselves or others, that one side of the question must be given up as untenable; those who are so convinced are bound to reject that which rests on testimony, not that which is supported by still existing facts. The very argument which Protestants have opposed to the doctrine of transubstantiation,* would, *if*

---

* The historian of the " Decline of the Roman Empire," carried the argument yet further ;—

" I still remember (he remarks) my solitary transport at " the discovery of a philosophical argument against tran- " substantiation ; that the text of Scripture which seems to " indicate the real presence is attested only by a single " sense—our sight ; while the real presence itself is disproved " by three of our senses—the sight, the touch, the taste."— *Gibbon's Memoirs of his Life*, vol. i. p. 58.

their view of the case were correct, be equally irresistible against the book of Genesis.

But let us consider what would be the conclusion of every reasonable being in a parallel case. Let us imagine a manuscript written three thousand years ago, and professing to be a revelation from the Deity, in which it was stated that the colour of the paper of the very book now in the reader's hands is *black*, and that the colour of the ink in the characters which he is now reading is *white :*—with that reasonable doubt of his own individual faculties which would become the inquirer into the truth of a statement said to be derived from so high an origin, he would ask of all those around him, whether to their senses the paper appeared to be *black* and the ink to be *white*. If he found the senses of other individuals agree with his own, then he would undoubtedly pronounce the alleged revelation a forgery, and those who propounded it to be either deceived or deceivers. He would rightly impute the attempted deceit to moral turpitude, to the gross ignorance or to the interested motives of the supporters of it ; and he certainly would not commit the impiety of supposing the Deity to have wrought a miraculous change upon the senses of our whole species, and to demand their belief in a fact directly opposed to those senses—thus throwing doubt upon every conclusion of reason which related to external objects, and amongst others, upon the very evidence by which the authenticity of that questionable manuscript was itself supported, and even of its very existence when before their eyes.

Thus, then, had those who attempt to show that the account of the creation, in the book of Genesis, is contradicted by the discoveries of modern science, succeeded, they would have destroyed the testimony of Moses—they would have uncanonised one portion of Scripture, and by implication have thrown doubt on the remainder. But minds which thus failed to trace out the necessary consequences of their own argument, were not likely to have laid very secure foundations for the basis on which it rested ; and I shall presently prove that the contradiction they have imagined can have no real existence ; and that whilst the testimony of Moses remains unimpeached, we may also be permitted to confide in the testimony of our senses.

CHAP. V.

FURTHER VIEW OF THE SAME SUBJECT.

BEFORE entering on the main argument it may be remarked, that the plainest and most natural view of the language employed by the sacred historian of the earth is, that his expressions ought to be received by us in the sense in which they were understood by the people to whom he addressed himself. If, when speaking of the creation, instead of using the terms light and water, he had spoken of the former as a wave, and of the latter as the union of two invisible airs, he would assuredly have been perfectly unintelligible to his country-men. At the distance of above three thousand years his writings would just have begun to be comprehended, and possibly three thousand years hence those views may be as inapplicable to the then existing state of human knowledge as they would have been when the first chapter of Genesis was written.

Those, however, who attempt to disprove the facts presented by observation, by placing them in opposition to revelation, have mistaken the very groundwork of the question. The revelation of Moses itself rests, and must necessarily rest, on *testimony*. Moses, the author of the oldest of the sacred books, lived about fifteen hundred years before the christian era, or about three thousand three hundred years ago. The oldest manuscripts of the Pentateuch at present known, appear to have been written about 900 years ago.* These were copied from

* Mr. Horne, in the *Introduction to the Critical Study of*

others of older date, and those again might probably, if their history were known, be traced up through a few transcripts to the original

the Holy Scriptures, states, that the total number of Hebrew MSS. collated by Dr. Kennicott, for his critical edition of the Hebrew Bible, was about 630. In that work, Mr. Horne gives an account of ten of the most ancient of these MSS. : three of which contain the first chapter of Genesis, viz. : —

No. 4. Codex Cæsenæ, in the Malatesta Library at Bologna, written about the end of the eleventh century.

No. 6. Codex Mediolanensis, written towards the close of the twelfth century. " The beginning of the book of " Genesis, and the end of Leviticus and Deuteronomy, " have been written by a later hand."

No. 8. Codex Parisiensis, 27, about the commencement of the twelfth century.

No. 10. Codex Parisiensis, 24, written at the beginning of the twelfth century.

In the same work is an account of six of the most ancient of the four hundred and seventy-nine collated by M. De Rossi. Two of these contain the first chapter of Genesis ; and the date of both is about the end of the eleventh or beginning of the twelfth century.

Of the Manuscripts of the Samaritan versions of the Pentateuch, cited in the same work—one the Codex 197, in the Ambrosian Library at Milan—Dr. Kennicott thinks that it is certainly not later than the tenth century.

author ; but no part of this is revelation ; it is testimony. Although the matter which the book contains was revealed to Moses, the fact that what we now receive as revelation is the same with that originally communicated revelation, is entirely dependent on testimony. Admitting, however, the full weight of that evidence, corroborated as it is by the Samaritan version ; nay, even supposing that we now possessed the identical autograph of the book of Genesis by the hand of its author, a most important question remains,—What means do we possess of translating it ?

In similar cases we avail ourselves of the works of the immediate predecessors, and of the contemporaries of the writer ; but here we are acquainted with no work of any prede-cessor,—of no writing of any contemporary ; and we do not possess the works of any writers in the same language, even during se-veral succeeding centuries, if we except some few of the sacred books. How, then, is it

possible to satisfy our minds of the minute
shades of meaning of words, perhaps employed
popularly; or, if they were employed in a
stricter and more philosophical sense, where
are the contemporary philosophical writings
from which their accurate interpretation may
be gained?

The extreme difficulty of such an inquiry
will be made apparent by imagining a parallel
case. Let us suppose all writings in the
English, and indeed in all other languages previous to the time of Shakespeare, to have been
destroyed;—let us imagine one manuscript of
his plays to remain, but not a vestige of the
works of any of his contemporaries; and further,
suppose the whole of the succeeding works of
English literature to be annihilated nearly up
to the present time. Under such circumstances,
what would be our knowledge of Shakespeare?
We should undoubtedly understand the general tenor and the plots of his plays. We
should *read* the language of all his characters;

and viewing it generally, we might even be said to understand it. But how many words connected with the customs, habits, and manners of the time must, under such circumstances, necessarily remain unknown to us! Still further, if any question arose, requiring for its solution a knowledge of the minute shades of meaning of words now long obsolete, or of terms supposed to be used in a strict or philosophical sense, how completely unsatisfactory must our conclusions remain! Such I conceive to be the view which common sense bids us take of the interpretation of the book of Genesis. The language of the Hebrews, in times long subsequent to the date of that book, may not have so far changed as to prevent us from rightly understanding generally the history it narrates; but there appears to be no reasonable ground for venturing to pronounce with confidence on the minute shades of meaning of allied words, and on such foundations to support an argument opposed to the evidence of our senses.

I should have hesitated in offering these remarks respecting the right interpretation of the Mosaic account of the creation, had the argument depended on any acquaintance with the language in which the sacred volume is written, or on any refinements of criticism, had I possessed that knowledge; but in estimating its validity, or in supplying a more cogent argument, I intreat the reader to consider well the difficulties which it is necessary to meet.

1st. The Church of England, if we may judge by the writings of those placed in authority, has hitherto considered it to have been expressly stated in the book of Genesis, that the earth was created about six thousand years ago.

2dly. Those observers and philosophers who have spent their lives in the study of Geology, have arrived at the conclusion that there exists irresistible evidence, that the date

of the earth's first formation is far anterior to
the epoch supposed to be assigned to it by
Moses; and it is now admitted by all compe-
tent persons, that the formation even of those
strata which are nearest the surface must have
occupied vast periods—probably millions of
years—in arriving at their present state.

3dly. Many of the most distinguished mem-
bers of the Church of England now distinctly
and formally admit the fact of such a lengthened existence of the earth we inhabit; for it
is so stated in the eighth *Bridgewater Treatise,*
a work written by the Professor of Geology in
the University of Oxford—himself holding an
office of dignity in that Church, and expressly
appointed to write upon that subject, by the
Archbishop of Canterbury, and the Bishop of
London.

4thly The Professor of Hebrew at the same
University has proposed a new interpretation
of those passages of the Book of Genesis,

which were hitherto supposed to be adverse to the now admitted facts.

Such being the present state of the case ;— it surely becomes a duty to require a very high degree of evidence, before we again claim authority for the opinion that the book of Genesis contains such a precise account of the work of the creation, that we may venture to appeal to it as a refutation of observed facts. The history of the past errors of our parent Church supplies us with a lesson of caution which ought not to be lost by its reformed successors. The fact that the venerable Galileo was compelled publicly to deny, on bended knee, a truth of which he had the most convincing demonstration, remains as a beacon to all after time, and ought not to be without its influence on the inquiring minds of the present day.

If the explanation offered by the Professor of Hebrew be admitted, those who adhere to it must still have some misgivings as to the effect of new discoveries in nature causing continual occasion for amended translations of various texts; whereas, should the view which has been advocated in this chapter be found correct, instead of fearing that the future progress of science may raise additional difficulties in the way of revealed religion, we are at once relieved from all doubt on that subject.

CHAP. VI.

OF THE DESIRE OF IMMORTALITY.

THAT wish, universally expressed in every variety of form, of remaining in the memory of our fellow-creatures after our passage from the present scene, has rightly been adduced as evidence of the desire of immortality, and has sometimes been explained as being founded on an instinctive belief that we are destined to it by the Creator.

The hope of remaining embalmed in the fond recollection of those we held most dear in life, and even of being remembered by our more immediate descendants, has something in it nearly connected with self; but the wish for more extended reputation,—the desire that our name should pass in after times from mouth to mouth, cherished and admired by those whose applause is won by no personal recollections : or the still more fervent aspirations, that we may stamp indelibly on the age we live in some mark of our individual existence which shall form an epoch in the history of man : these hopes, these longings, receive no interpretation from the all-dominant principle of *self;* unless indeed we suppose the sentient principle of our nature not merely existing, but also conscious of, and gratified by, the earthly immortality it had achieved. Yet the more distant and the higher the objects we pursue, the less is it possible to suppose the mind, so occupied on earth, can, in another stage of its existence, derive pleasure from such perceptions.

To support this opinion, it is only necessary

G 2

to examine the states of mind in the various classes of the aspirants after fame .

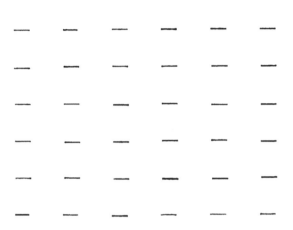

Through every form of society, and through every rank of each, may be traced this universal passion. Examine the most highly civilized inhabitants of earth ; search through it for the most cultivated and refined in taste ; for the most sagacious in penetrating the passions of mankind, the most skilful in wielding them, or the most powerful in intellectual might. Taste, feeling, passion, ambition, genius, severed or combined, equally yield obedience to its sway, and present, under different appearances, the effects of its all-controlling power.

— — — — — —

— — — — — —

— — — — — —

— — — — — —

— — — — — —

— — — — — —

Look at the highest productions of the poet or the novelist. By connecting his story with the scenery, the traditions, or the history of his country, he may ensure for it a local inte-rest, a domestic and transitory popularity; but it is that deeper penetration into the secrets of the human heart, which enables him to select from amongst the same materials, those feelings that are common to the race which have, as occasion called them forth, appeared, and will continue to reappear, as long as the same affections and passions shall continue to animate and agitate our frames.

From the examination of these its highest forms, we may gather some common principles, and be enabled to perceive that the love of fame is far different from that passion for vulgar applause with which it is too frequently confounded. We may learn, that the higher the intellectual powers devoted to the task, the more remote the period for which ambition delights to raise its far distant altar.

CHAP. VII.

ON TIME.

Time and change are great, only with reference to the faculties of the beings which
note them. The insect of an hour, which
flutters, during its transient existence, in an
atmosphere of perfume, would attribute un-
changing duration to the beautiful flowers
of the cistus, whose petals cover the dewy

grass but a few hours after it has received the lifeless body of the gnat. These flowers, could they reflect, might contrast their transitory lives with the prolonged existence of their greener neighbours. The leaves themselves, counting their brief span by the lapse of a few moons, might regard as almost indefinitely extended the duration of the common parent of both leaf and flower. The lives of individual trees are lost in the continued destruction and renovation which take place in forest masses. Forests themselves, starved by the exhaustion of the soil, or consumed by fire, succeed each other in slow gradation. A forest of oaks waves its luxuriant branches over a spot which has been fertilized by the ashes of a forest of pines. These periods again merge into other and still longer cycles, during which the latest of a thousand forests sinks beneath the waves, from the gradual subsidence of its parent earth ; or in which extensive inundations, by accumulating the silt of centuries, gradually convert the

living trunks into their stony resemblances.
Stratum upon stratum subsides in comminuted
particles, and is accumulated in the depths of
the ocean, whence they again arise, consolidated by pressure or by fire, to form the continents and mountains of a new creation.

Such, in endless succession, is the history of
the changes of the globe we dwell upon ; and
human observation, aided by human reason,
has as yet discovered few signs of a beginning—no symptom of an end. Yet, in
that more extended view which recognises
our planet as one amongst the attendants of
a central luminary ; that sun itself the soul,
as it were, of vegetable and animal existence,
but an insignificant individual among its
congeners of the milky way :—when we remember that that cloud of light, gleaming
with its myriad systems, is but an isolated
nebula amongst a countless host of rivals,
which the starry firmament surrounding us
on all sides, presents to us in every varied

form;—some as uncondensed masses of attenuated light;—some as having, in obedience
to attractive forces, assumed a spherical figure;
others, as if farther advanced in the history of
their fate, having a denser central nucleus
surrounded by a more diluted light, spreading
into such vast spaces, that the whole of our
own nebula would be lost in it :—others there
are, in which the apparently unformed and
irregular mass of nebulous light is just curd-
ling, as it were, into separate systems; whilst
many present a congeries of distinct points of
light, each, perhaps, the separate luminary of
a creation more glorious than our own ;—when
the birth, the progress, and the history of
sidereal systems are considered, we require
some other unit of time than even that comprehensive one which astronomy has unfolded
to our view. Minute and almost infinitesimal
as is the time which comprises the history of
our race compared with that which records
the history of our system, the space even of

this latter period forms too limited a standard wherewith to measure the footmarks of
eternity.

CHAP. VIII.

ARGUMENT FROM LAWS INTERMITTING ON THE NATURE OF MIRACLES.

THE object of the present chapter is to show that miracles are not deviations from the laws assigned by the Almighty for the government of matter and of mind; but that they are the exact fulfilment of much more extensive laws than those we suppose to exist. In fact, if we were endued with acuter senses and higher reasoning faculties, they are the very points we should seek to observe, as the test of any hypothesis we had been led to frame concerning the nature of those laws. Even with our present imperfect faculties we frequently arrive at the highest confirmation of our views of the laws of nature, by tracing their actions under *singular* circumstances.

The mode by which.I propose to arrive at these conclusions is, by appealing to the judgment which each individual will himself form, when examining that piece of mere human mechanism, to which the argument so frequently compels me to advert. If he shall agree with me, that the second of the two views presented to him exhibits a higher degree of knowledge, and a higher exertion of power, than the first, he must inevitably conclude, that the view here taken of the nature of a miracle, assigns a far higher degree of power and knowledge to the Deity.

Let the reader again imagine himself sitting before the calculating engine, and let him again observe and ascertain, by lengthened

induction, the nature of the law it is com-
puting.   Let him imagine that he has seen
the changes wrought on its face by the lapse of
thousands of years, and that, without one solitary exception, he has found the engine register the series of square numbers. Suppose,
now, the maker of that machine to say to the
observer, " I will, by moving a certain mecha-
" nism, which is invisible to you, cause the
" engine to make a cube number instead of a
" square one, and then to revert to its former
" course of square numbers;" the observer would
be inclined to attribute to him a degree of
power but little superior to that which was
necessary to form the original engine.

But, let the same observer, after the same
lapse of time—the same amount of uninterrupted experience of the uniformity of the law
of square numbers, hear the maker of that engine say to him— " The next number which
" shall appear on those wheels, and which
" you expect to find a square number, shall

" not be such. When the machine was ori-
" ginally ordered to make these calculations,
" I impressed on it a law, which should coin-
" cide with that of square numbers in every
" case, *except* the one which is now about to
" appear, after which no future exception can
" ever occur; but the unvarying law of the
" squares shall be pursued until the machine
" itself perishes from decay."

Undoubtedly the observer would ascribe a
greater degree of power to the artist who thus
willed that event at the distance of ages before
its arrival.

If the contriver of the engine then explain
to him, that, by the very structure of it, he has
power to order any number of such apparent
deviations from its laws to occur at any future
periods, however remote, and that each of
these may be of a different kind ; and, if he
also inform him, that he gave it that structure
in order to meet events, which he foresaw must

happen at those respective periods, there can be no doubt that the observer would ascribe to the inventor far higher knowledge than if, when those events severally occurred, he were to intervene, and temporarily alter the calculations of the machine.

If, besides this, he were so far to explain the structure of the engine that the observer could himself, by some simple process, such as the mere moving of a bolt, call into action those apparent deviations whenever certain combinations were presented to his eye; if he were thus to impart a power of predicting such excepted cases, dependent on the will, although otherwise beyond the limits of the observer's power and knowledge, such a structure would be admitted as evidence of a still more skilful contrivance.

The engine which, in a former chapter, I introduced to the reader, possesses these powers. It may be set, so as to obey by any

given law; and, at any periods, however remote, to make one or more *seeming* exceptions
to that law. It is, however, to be observed,
that the *apparent* law which the spectator arrived at, by an almost unlimited induction, is
not the full expression of the law by which the
machine acts; and that the excepted case is
as absolutely and irresistibly the necessary
consequence of its primitive adjustment, as is
any individual calculation amongst the countless multitude.

When the construction of that engine was
first attempted, I did not seek to give to it
the power of making calculations so far beyond the reach of mathematical analysis as
these appear to be: nor can I now foresee
a probable period at which they may become
practically available to human wants. I had
determined to invest the invention with a degree of generality which should include a wide
range of mathematical power; and I was well
aware that the mechanical generalisations

I had organised contained within them much more than I had leisure to study, and some things which will probably remain unproductive to a far distant day.

Amongst those combinations which I was induced to examine, I observed the powers I have now recorded; and the reflections they produced in my own mind, impelled me to pursue them for a time. If the reader agree with me in opinion, that these speculations have led to a more exalted view of the great Author of the universe than any we yet possessed, he must also have arrived at the conclusion, that the study of the most abstract branch of practical mechanics, combined with that of the most abstruse portions of mathematical science, has no tendency to incapacitate the human mind from the perception of the evidences of natural religion; and that even those very sources themselves furnish arguments which have opened more splendid views of the grandeur of creation than any which the sciences

of observation or of physics have yet supplied.

It may not, perhaps, be without its use to
suggest another illustration respecting the nature of miracles. It is known that mathematical laws are sometimes expressed by curves.
The figure 1 represents a re-entering curve of
four dimensions, whose law of formation is
given in the note.* A slight change in the nature of the constants makes it assume the form
of fig. 2, which is still a continuous curve ; but
a further change of the constants causes it to
have two ovals, quite disconnected from the
larger portion ; and, as the constants again
alter, these ovals are reduced to points.

---

* The equation
$$y^4 - 4 y^2 = - ax^4 + bx^3 + cx^2 + dx + e$$
expresses several figures of an oval form, according to the
nature of the roots of the equation,
$$- ax^4 + bx^3 + cx^2 + dx + e = o.$$
If its two lesser roots become imaginary, the curves, figures
1, 2, 3, are produced.

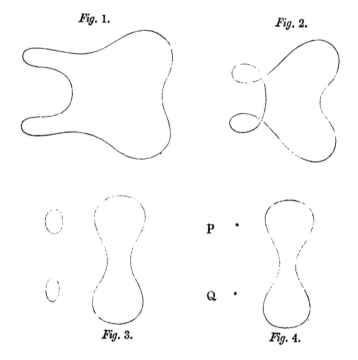

Fig. 1.　Fig. 2.

Fig. 3.　Fig. 4.

P

Q

In all four cases, every point in each branch
of the curve obeys the same general law.   The
points, P and Q, invisible to the eye, are yet
detected by mathematical analysis, and fulfil
as precisely the original equation as any of the
infinite number of other points, which constitute the rest of the curve.   These points might
be situated on the curve itself, and they are
well known to mathematicians.   It is to these
singular points, which really fulfil the law of
the curve, but which present to those who
only judge of them by the organ of sight
an apparent discontinuity, that I wish to
call the attention, as offering an illustration
of the doctrine here explained respecting
miracles.

It has been remarked, in the beginning of
the present chapter, that it is to the singular
points—to those points of such infinitely rare
occurrence in a curve—that we frequently have
recourse, as the test of our theories, for explaining the phenomena of nature.

The existence, under peculiar circumstances,
of conical refraction, was predicted by Sir W.
Hamilton ; and, from an analytical investigation into the nature of the curve surface, which
represents the form of the luminiferous wave
within the crystal, he ascertained that it had
four conoidal cusps, at each of which there were,
consequently, an infinite number of tangent
planes. The course of the refracted ray being
determined by the tangent plane to the wave
surface, it followed that a single ray within the
crystal, transmitted in the direction of the line
joining two opposite cusps, corresponded to an
infinite number of refracted rays without, constituting a refracted cone.

The second case of conical refraction, predicted by Sir William Hamilton, depended on
another mathematical fact—namely, that the
wave surface is touched in an infinite number
of points, constituting a small circle of contact,
by a single plane parallel to one of the circu-
lar sections of the surface of elasticity.

Professor Lloyd undertook to make the very delicate experiments required for this most interesting subject. Of the great importance of this investigation, Professor Lloyd was fully aware, for he remarks—

" Here, then, are two singular and unex-
" pected consequences of the undulatory theory,
" not only unsupported by any facts hitherto
" observed, but even opposed to all the analo-
" gies derived from experience. If confirmed
" by experiment, they would furnish new and
" almost convincing proofs of that theory;
" and, if disproved, on the other hand, it is
" evident that the theory must be abandoned
" or modified.*

On examining the first of these cases, experimentally, the fact of conical refraction was fully established. But a new result now presented itself: the rays of light thus conically

* Trans. of Royal Irish Academy, Vol. XVII.

refracted were found to be polarized; and it
was observed, that "the angle between the
"planes of polarization of any two rays of
"the cone was half the angle between the
"planes, containing the rays themselves, and
"the axis."

This new law, thus approximately obtained
by experiment, led the observer back to the
theory; and, on a further examination, he detected in that theory the very law he had just
discovered by observation.

The second case of conical refraction required experiments of a still more delicate
nature.   They were, however, made, and succeeded equally.   The conically refracted ray
was found to be polarised, according to the law
which, in this instance, analysis had predicted;
and, to complete the triumph of this union of
theory and experiment, the measures in both
cases, when made under proper circumstances,
accorded with the theoretical conclusions,

within such limits as might be fairly attributed to the necessary errors of observation.

It is worthy of remark, that, at first, two facts presented themselves, which seemed at variance with the theory. In the first place, the emergent rays formed a solid cone, instead of a conical surface ; and, in the second place, the calculated angle, subtended by the sides of the cone, was only one half the observed angle. Both the facts were shown to depend upon the size of the aperture, and to arise from the rays which were inclined at small angles to the single theoretical direction. When the aperture was diminished, so as to be *very* small, (the case calculated by Sir William Hamilton,) then the cone of light became a conical surface, and the observed angle was the same as the calculated one.*

* Those who are acquainted with the history of astronomy, cannot fail to recall a parallel discrepancy between observation and calculation in the theory of gravity. It appeared to result from that law, that the motion of the moon's

apogee was only one half of what observation proved it to be ;
and it is singular that Euler, D'Alembert, and Clairaut
arrived, by different methods, at the same erroneous result ;
and the truth of the great law of gravity appeared for a time
to be doubtful. Clairaut, however, having assumed that
the law of gravity contained a term only sensible at small
distances (such as that of the moon), re-calculated the question, and finding it necessary, in consequence of this term, to
push his approximation further than he had done, arrived
at the conclusion, that the co-efficient of the new term va-
nished ; and also, that the simple law of the inverse square
of the distance, when the approximations were sufficiently
pursued, gave the whole motions which observations had
discovered.

CHAP. IX.

ON THE PERMANENT IMPRESSION OF OUR WORDS AND ACTIONS ON THE GLOBE WE INHABIT.

THE principle of the equality of action and reaction, when traced through all its consequences, opens views which will appear to many persons most unexpected.

The pulsations of the air, once set in motion by the human voice, cease not to exist with the sounds to which they gave rise. Strong and audible as they may be in the immediate neighbourhood of the speaker, and at the immediate moment of utterance, their quickly attenuated force soon becomes inaudible to human ears. The motions they have impressed on the particles of one portion of our atmosphere, are communicated to constantly increasing numbers, but the quantity of motion measured in the same direction receives no addition. Each atom loses as much as it gives, and regains again from others, portions of those motions which they in turn give up.

The waves of air thus raised, perambulate the earth and ocean's surface, and in less than twenty hours every atom of its atmosphere takes up the altered movement due to that infinitesimal portion of the primitive motion which has been conveyed to it through countless channels, and which must continue to influence its path throughout its future existence.*

* La courbe décrite par une simple molécule d'air ou vapeurs est réglée d'une manière aussi certain que les orbites planétaires : il n'y a de différence entre elles, que

But these aerial pulses, unseen by the keenest eye, unheard by the acutest ear, unperceived by human senses, are yet demonstrated to exist by human reason ; and, in some few and limited instances, by calling to our aid the most refined and comprehensive instrument of human thought, their courses are traced and their intensities are measured. If man enjoyed a larger command over mathematical analysis, his knowledge of these motions would be more extensive ; but a being possessed of the unbounded knowledge of that science, would trace every the minutest consequences of that primary impulse. Such a being, however far exalted above our race, would yet be immeasurably below even our conception of infinite intelligence ; yet by him, supposing the original conditions of each atom of the atmosphere, as well as all the extraneous causes acting upon it to be given, its future and inevitable path would be clearly traced ; and

celle qu'y met notre ignorance.—*La Place, Théorie Analytique des Probabilités.* Int. p. iv.

supposing the interference also of no new causes, the circumstances of the future history of the whole of the earth's atmosphere would be distinctly seen, and might be absolutely predicted for any even the remotest point of time. *

Let us imagine a being, invested with such knowledge, to arrive at the predicted moment. If any the slightest deviation exists, he will immediately read in its existence the action of a new cause; and, through the aid of the same analysis, tracing this discordance back to its source, he would become aware of the time of its commencement, and the point of space at which it originated.

Thus considered, what a strange chaos is this wide atmosphere we breathe! Every atom impressed with good and with ill, retains at once the motions which philosophers

* See Note C in the Appendix.

and sages have imparted to it, mixed and combined in ten thousand ways with all that is worthless and base. The air itself is one vast library, on whose pages are for ever written all that man has ever said or even whispered. There, in their mutable but unerring characters, mixed with the earliest, as well as the latest sighs of mortality, stand for ever recorded, vows unredeemed, promises unfulfilled, perpetuating in the united movements of each particle, the testimony of man's changeful will.

But if the air we breathe is the never-failing historian of the sentiments we have uttered, earth, air, and ocean, are in like manner the eternal witnesses of the acts we have done. The same principle of the equality of action and reaction applies to them : whatever motion is communicated to any of their particles, is transmitted to all around it, the share of each being diminished by their number, and depending jointly on the number and position of those

I

acted upon by the original source of disturbance.
The waves of air, although in many instances
sensible to the organs of hearing, are only rendered visible to the eye by peculiar contrivances; whilst those of water offer to the sense
of sight the most beautiful illustration of the
transmission of motion. Every one who has
thrown a pebble into the still waters of a sheltered pool, has seen the circles it has raised
gradually expanding in size, and as uniformly
diminishing in distinctness. He may have observed the reflection of those waves from the
edges of the pool. He may also have noticed
the perfect distinctness with which two, three,
or more series of waves each pursues its own
unimpeded course, when diverging from two,
three, or more centres of disturbance. He may
have observed, that in such cases the particles
of water where the waves intersect each other,
partake of the movements due to each series.

No motion impressed by natural causes, or
by human agency, is ever obliterated. The

ripple on the ocean's surface caused by a gentle
breeze, or the still water which marks the more
immediate track of a ponderous vessel gliding
with scarcely expanded sails over its bosom,
are equally indelible. The momentary waves
raised by the passing gale, apparently born but
to die on the spot which saw their birth, leave
behind them an endless progeny, which, reviv-
ing with diminished energy in other seas, and
visiting a thousand shores, reflected from each
and perhaps again partially concentrated, pursue
their ceaseless course till ocean be itself annihilated.

The track of every canoe, of every vessel
which has yet disturbed the surface of the
ocean, whether impelled by manual force or
elemental power, remains for ever registered
in the future movement of all succeeding particles which may occupy its place. The furrow
which it left is, indeed, instantly filled up by
the closing waters; but they draw after them
other and larger portions of the surrounding

element, and these again once moved, communicate motion to others in endless succession.

The solid substance of the globe itself, whether we regard the minutest movement of the soft clay which receives its impression from the foot of animals, or the concussion produced from falling mountains rent by earthquakes, equally retains and communicates, through all its countless atoms, their apportioned shares of the motions so impressed.

Whilst the atmosphere we breathe is the ever-living witness of the sentiments we have uttered, the waters, and the more solid materials of the globe, bear equally enduring testimony of the acts we have committed.

If the Almighty stamped on the brow of the earliest murderer,—the indelible and visible mark of his guilt,—he has also established laws by which every succeeding criminal is not less irrevocably chained to the testimony of his crime ; for every atom of his mortal frame, through whatever changes its severed particles may migrate, will still retain, adhering to it through every combination, some movement derived from that very muscular effort, by which the crime itself was perpetrated.

CHAP. X.

ON HUME'S ARGUMENT AGAINST MIRACLES.

FEW arguments have excited greater attention, and produced more attempts at refutàtion,
than the celebrated one of David Hume, respecting miracles; and it might be added,
that more sophistry has been advanced against
it, than its author employed in the whole of his
writings.

It must be admitted that in the argument, as
originally developed by its author, there exists
some confusion between personal experience
and that which is derived from testimony; and
that there are several other points open to
criticism and objection; but the main argu-

ment, divested of its less important adjuncts, never has, and never will be refuted. Dr. Johnson seems to have been of this opinion, as the following extract from his life by Boswell proves :—

" Talking of Dr. Johnson's unwillingness to believe ex-traordinary things, I ventured to say—

" ' Sir, you come near to Hume's argument against mira-' cles—That it is more probable witnesses should lie, or be ' mistaken, than that they should happen.'

" Johnson.—' Why, Sir, Hume, taking the proposition ' simply, is right. But the Christian revelation is not proved ' by miracles alone, but as connected with prophecies, and ' with the doctrines in confirmation of which miracles were ' wrought.' "*

Hume contends that a miracle is a violation of the laws of nature; and as a firm and unalterable experience has established these laws, the proof against a miracle from the very nature of the fact, is as entire as any argument from experience can possibly be imagined.

* Boswell's Life of Johnson. Oxford, 1826. vol. iii. p. 169.

" The plain consequence is (and it is a general maxim
" worthy of our attention), that no testimony is sufficient
" to establish a miracle, unless the testimony be of such a
" kind, that its falsehood would be more miraculous than the
" fact which it endeavours to establish : and even in that case
" there is a mutual destruction of arguments, and the superior
" only gives us an assurance suitable to that degree of force
" which remains after deducting the inferior." *

The difficulty which is frequently experi-
enced in understanding this argument, appears
to arise from the circumstance, that a double
negative is concealed under the words " *its
falsehood would be more miraculous than.*" For
in Hume's argument the word " *miraculous*"
means *improbable*, although the improbability
is of a very high degree. The clause then
reads—

Its *falsehood* would be *more improbable* than

which is evidently equivalent to

Its *truth* would be *less* improbable than ;

which is again equivalent to

Its *truth* would be *more probable* than.

---

* Hume's Essays, Edinburgh, 1817, vol. ii. p. 117.

Replacing this in Hume's argument, it stands thus—

" That no testimony is sufficient to establish a miracle,
" unless the testimony be of such a kind, that its *truth*
" would be *more probable* than the fact which it endea-
" vours to establish.

The argument is now reduced to the mere truism, that—

The *probability* in favour of the testimony by which a miracle is supported, must be *greater* than the *probability* of the miracle itself.

Before entering on the arguments I have to offer upon this point, it will be right to recall to the reader the view taken in a preceding chapter concerning the nature of miracles, and to compare it with that entertained by the acute philosopher whose essay I am venturing to criticise, lest, from any unperceived differ-ence in the employment of the term, I should inadvertently mislead both myself and my readers.

It has been shown in the chapter above referred to, that—*A miracle may be only the exact fulfilment of a general law of nature, under such singular circumstances that to those imperfectly acquainted with that law, it appears to be in direct opposition to it.* The definition of a miracle adopted by Hume is this—

" A miracle is a violation of the laws of nature." *

And again, in note K—

" A miracle may be accurately defined—*A transgression* " *of a law of nature by a particular volition of the Deity, or* " *by the interposition of some invisible agent.* A miracle may " be either discovered by men or not. This alters not its " essence or its nature."†

In order rightly to interpret this definition of a miracle, it is necessary to have the author's definition of a law of nature, which is given in a subsequent part of his essay.

" It is experience only which gives authority to human " testimony ; and it is the same experience which assures us

* Page 114.   † Page 462.

" of the laws of nature. When, therefore, these two kinds
" of experience are contrary, we have nothing to do but
" subtract the one from the other, and embrace an opinion,
" either on one side or the other, with that assurance which
" arises from the remainder."*

Having pointed out the difference in our definitions, I shall now show a point of resemblance between them, which is apparent in the following extract—

" What we have said of miracles, may be applied without
" any variation to prophecies; and indeed *all prophecies are*
" *real miracles*, and as such only can be admitted as proofs
" of any revelation."†

The reader who has entered into the reasoning of Chapter VIII. of this fragment will perceive that, according to the views there maintained, it might be asserted that all miracles are prophecies: that they are revelations more or less in advance of events which, although in real accordance, are apparently in direct contradiction to the laws of nature.

---

* Hume's Essay, vol. ii. p. 129.

† Page 131. A passage in this quotation has for convenience been marked in italics; it is not so in the original.

Hume's argument in the first part of the Essay of Miracles, seems intended to prove that although the Deity might cause miracles to be worked, yet that it is impossible that those who did not witness them, could be convinced of their having occurred by any human testimony.

In the second part of that essay the author applies a limitation to which he requests particular attention—namely, that no human testimony can have such force as to prove a miracle, *and make it a just foundation for any system of religion.*

" I beg the limitations here made may be remarked, " when I say, that a miracle can never be proved, so as to " be the foundation of a system of religion."*

Had the argument been continued, it might have *appeared* still more startling; for, as all miracles of which we have any account, rest, in

* Hume's Essay, vol. ii. p. 128.

the first instance, on the testimony of eye-witnesses who are not themselves alive to deliver
their testimony, we require the fact that they
did so testify, to be confirmed to us by the testimony of others. Now, if, in order to prove
the miracle, it must be a greater miracle that
the testimony of the eye-witnesses is **true** ; so,
in order to assure us that the eye-witnesses did
testify it, it must be a still greater miracle that
those who assure us of that fact, themselves
speak the truth. If this second testimony is not
communicated to us personally, but is again
transmitted, either through persons or through
writings, we must again, at each transmission,
require a greater miracle than at the preceding.
Thus, it might at first sight be made to appear,
that the amount of evidence required to establish the truth of a miracle, said to have been
performed at any distant period of past time,
would be enormous.

However alarming this doctrine may appear,
an examination of the real *numerical* value of

the quantities spoken of in Hume's argument as greater and less, will prove, as has frequently happened in other instances, that the consequences deduced from it by no means *necessarily* follow.

Hume has deduced the *à priori* probability against the occurrence of a miracle, from the universal experience of mankind; and, as it is only our own entire ignorance of all their causes which renders the question of miracles one of probability, there is no objection to be made to this step. On the contrary, it enables us to lay the foundation of numerical deductions, which have none of the vagueness of those at which Hume arrived.

Taking, therefore, Hume's own mode of estimating a miracle, let us suppose the chances against its occurrence to be n to 1, where n is some enormously large number. Still, however, in this view of the question, there is a probability, however small, for its occurrence,

whilst there exists an improbability of vast magnitude against it,   It is on this ground that I
have, according to Hume's own notions, called
a *miracle* an *improbability ;* and we may, therefore, substitute that term for miracle and miraculous.   The argument of Hume, when so
translated, stands thus :—

*That no testimony is sufficient to establish an
improbability, unless the testimony be of such a
kind that its falsehood would be more improbable than the occurrence of the fact which it endeavours to establish.*

But the " fact which it endeavours to establish" is the improbability mentioned in the
second line.   Consequently, the testimony
must be of such a nature, that its falsehood
would be more improbable than that first improbability.

Let us now apply the test of number to the
argument of Hume ; and, for the sake of simpli-

city, let us take the case of the miracle mentioned in the next chapter, and let us assume
that the improbability that a dead person will
be restored to life, as deduced from past experience, is 200,000,000,000 to 1.

Let us also suppose that there are witnesses
who will speak the truth, and who are not themselves deceived in ninety-nine cases out of a
hundred. Now, let us examine what is the
probability of the falsehood of a statement in
which two such persons absolutely unknown
to and unconnected with each other agree.

Since the order in which independent witnesses give their testimony does not affect their
credit, we may suppose that, in a given number of statements, both witnesses tell the truth
in the ninety-nine first cases, and the falsehood in the hundredth. Then,

The first time the second witness B testifies,
he will agree with the testimony of the first

witness A, in the ninety-nine first cases, and differ from him in the hundredth. Similarly, in the second testimony of B, he will again agree with A in ninety-nine cases, and differ in the hundredth, and so on for ninety-nine times; so that, after A has testified a hundred, and B ninety-nine times, we shall have

99 × 99 cases in which both agree,
 99 cases in which they differ, A being wrong.

Now, in the hundredth case in which B testifies, he is wrong; and, if we combine this with the testimony of A, we have ninety-nine cases in which A is right and B wrong; and one case only in which both A and B agree in error. The whole number of cases, which amounts to ten thousand, may be thus divided :—

99 × 99 = 9801 cases in which A and B agree in truth,
 1 × 99 = 99 cases in which B is true and A false,
99 × 1 = 99 cases in which A is true and B false,
 1 × 1 =   1 case in which both A and B agree in a
         falsehood.
 _____
  10,000 cases.

K

As there is only one case in ten thousand
in which two such independent witnesses can
agree in error, the probability of their testimony
being false is $\frac{1}{10,000}$ or $\frac{1}{(100)^2}$.

The reader will already perceive how great
a reliance is due to the concurring testimony
of two independent witnesses of tolerably good
character and understanding. It appears that
the chance of one such witness being in error
is $\frac{1}{(100)}$; that of two concurring in the same
error is $\frac{1}{(100)^2}$; and if the same reasoning be applied to three independent witnesses, it will be
found that the probability of their agreeing in
error is $\frac{1}{(100)^3}$; or that the odds are 999,999 to
1 against the agreement.

Pursuing the same reasoning, the probability
of the falsehood of a fact which six such independent witnesses attest is $\frac{1}{(100)^6}$ or it is, in
round numbers,

1,000,000,000,000 to 1 against the falsehood of their testimony.

The improbability of the miracle of a dead
man being restored, is, as we have seen, on the
principles stated by Hume, $\frac{1}{20\,(100)^5}$; or it is—

200,000,000,000 to 1 against its occurrence.

It follows, then, that the improbability of the
falsehood of the concurring testimony of only
six such independent witnesses, is already *five
times* as great as the improbability against the
miracle of a dead man's being restored to life,
deduced from Hume's method of estimating
its probability solely from experience. As the
argument of Hume is universal, it is sufficient
for its refutation to give a single instance in
which it does not hold.

The reader will find, in a note in the Appendix, the mathematical inquiry, in which, the
degree of improbability of the miracle and

K 2

the degree of probability belonging to the witnesses being assigned, it will be seen whether any, and what number of such witnesses, can outweigh the improbability of the miracle.

CHAP. XI.

À PRIORI ARGUMENT IN FAVOUR OF THE OCCUR-RENCE OF MIRACLES.

In the present chapter it is proposed to prove, that—

It is more probable that any law, at the knowledge of which we have arrived by observation, shall be subject to one of those violations which, according to Hume's definition, constitutes a miracle, than that it should not be so subjected.

To show the probability of this, we may be allowed again to revert to the Calculating Engine : and to assume that it is possible to set the machine, so that it shall calculate *any*

algebraic law whatever : and also possible so to
arrange it, that at any periods, *however remote,*
the first law shall be interrupted for one or
more times, and be superseded by *any other
law ;* after which the original law shall again
be produced, and no other deviation shall ever
take place.

Now, as all laws, which appear to us regular
and uniform in their course, and to be subject
to no exception, can be calculated by the engine: and as each of these laws may also be
calculated by the same machine, subject to any
assigned interruption, at distinct and definite
periods ; each simple law may be interrupted at
any point by a portion of any one of all the
other simple laws : it follows, that *the class of
laws subject to interruption is far more extensive
than that of laws which are uninterrupted.* It
is, in fact, infinitely more numerous. Therefore, the probability of any law with which we
have become acquainted by observation being
part of a much more extensive law, and having,

to use mathematical language, singular points
or discontinuous functions contained within it,
is very large.

Perhaps it may be objected, that the laws
calculated by such an engine are not laws of
nature, and that any deviation from laws produced by human mechanism does not come
within Hume's definition of miracles.   To this
it may be answered, that a law of nature has
been defined by Hume to rest upon experience, or repeated observation, just as the truth
of testimony does.   Now, the law produced by
the engine may be arrived at by precisely the
same means — namely, repeated observation.

It may, however, be desirable to explain
further the nature of that evidence, on which
the fact, that the engine possesses those powers,
rests.

When the Calculating Engine has been set
to compute the successive terms of any given

law, which the observer is told will have an apparent exception (at, for example, the ten million and twenty-third term,) the observer is directed to note down the commencement of its computations; and, by comparing these results with his own independent calculations of the same law, he may verify the accuracy of the engine as far as he chooses. It may then be demonstrated to him, by the very structure of the machine, that if its motion were continued, it would, *necessarily*, at the end of a very long time, arrive at the ten-millionth term of the law assigned to it ; and that, by an equal *necessity*, it would have passed through all the intermediate terms. The inquirer is now desired to turn on the wheels with his own hand, until they are precisely in the same situation as they would have been had the engine itself gone on continuously, to the ten-millionth term. The machine is again put in motion, and the observer again finds that each successive term it calculates fulfils the original law. But, after passing twenty-two terms, he now observes *one* term which does not fulfil the original law, but which does coincide with the predicted exception.

The continued movement now again produces terms according with the first law, and the observer may continue to verify them as long as he wishes. It may then be demonstrated to him, by the very structure of the machine, that, if its motion were continued, it would be *impossible* that any other deviation from the apparent law could ever occur at any future time.

Such is the evidence to the observer; and, if the superintendent of the engine were, at his request, to make it calculate a great variety of different laws, each interrupted by special and remote exceptions, he would have ample ground to believe in the assertion of its director, that he could so arrange the engine that any law, however complicated, might be calculated to any assigned extent, when there should arise one apparent exception; after which the original law should continue uninterrupted for ever.

Let us now consider the miracle alluded to by Hume—the restoration of a dead man to life. According to the definition of that author, our belief in such a fact being contrary to the laws of nature, arises from our uniform experience against it. Our personal experience is small : we must therefore have recourse to testimony; and from that we learn, that the dead are *never* restored to life ; and, consequently, we have the uniform experience of all mankind since the creation, against one assigned instance of a dead man being so restored. Let us now find the numerical amount of this evidence. Assuming the origin of the human race to have been about six thousand years ago, and taking thirty years as the duration of a generation, we have—

$$\frac{6000}{30} = 200 \text{ generations.}$$

And allowing that the average population of the earth has been a thousand millions, we find that there have been born and have died since the creation,

$$200 \times 1,000,000,000$$
$$=200,000,000,000 \text{ individuals.}$$

Such, then, according to Hume, are the odds against the truth of the miracle : that is to say, it is found from experience, that it is about two hundred thousand millions to one against a dead man having been restored to life.

Let us now compare this with a parallel case in the calculations of the engine ; and let us suppose the number above stated to be a hundred million times as great, or that the truth of the miracles is opposed by a number of instances, expressed by twenty places of figures.

The engine may be set to count the natural numbers—1, 2, 3, 4, &c. ; and it shall continue

to fulfil that law, not merely for the number of
times just mentioned, for that number is quite
insignificant among the vast periods it involves ;
but the natural numbers shall follow in continual succession, until they have reached an
amount which requires for its expression above
a hundred million places of figures. If every
letter in the volume now before the reader's
eyes were changed into a figure, and if all the
figures contained in a thousand such volumes
were arranged in order, the whole together
would yet fall far short of the vast induction
the observer would have had in favour of the
truth of the law of natural numbers. The
widest range of all the cycles of astronomy and
geology combined, sink into insignificance before such a period.   Yet, shall the engine, true
to the prediction of its director, after the lapse
of myriads of ages, fulfil its task, and give
that one, the *first* and *only* exception to
that time-sanctioned law.   What would have
been the chances against the appearance of
the excepted case, immediately prior to its

occurrence ? It would have had, according to Hume, the evidence of all experience against it, with a force myriads of times more strong than that against any miracle.

Now, let the reader, who has fully entered into the nature of the argument, ask himself this question :—Does he believe that such an engine has really been contrived, and what reasonable grounds has he for that belief?

The testimony of any single witness is small against such odds ; besides, the witness may deceive himself. Whether he speaks truly, will be estimated by his moral character—whether he deceives himself, will be estimated by his intellectual character. The probability that such an engine has been contrived, will, however, receive great addition, when it is remarked, that mathematical—and, especially, geometrical evidence is, of all others, that in which the fewest mistakes arise, and in which they are most readily discovered ; and when it is added, that the fact of the invention of such an engine may be deduced from the drawings with all the force of demonstration, and that it rests on precisely the same species of evidence as the propositions of Euclid. Whether such an engine could be actually made in the present state of mechanical art, is a question of quite a different order : it must rest upon the opinions of those who have had extensive experience in that art. The author has not the slightest hesitation in stating his opinion to be, that it is fully within those limits.

This, however, is a question foreign to the nature of the argument, which might have been stated in a more abstract manner, without any reference to such an engine. As, however, it really arose from that machine, and as visible forms make a much deeper impression on the mind than any abstract reasonings, it has been stated in conjunction with that subject.

CHAPTER XII.

THOUGHTS ON THE NATURE OF FUTURE PUNISHMENTS.

WHO has not felt the painful memory of departed folly? who has not at times found crowding on his recollection, thoughts, feelings, scenes, by all perhaps but him forgotten, which force themselves involuntarily on his attention? Who has not reproached himself with the bitterest regret at the follies he has thought, or said, or acted? Time brings no alleviation to these periods of morbid memory : the weaknesses of our youthful days, as well as those of later life, come equally

unbidden and unarranged, to mock our attention and claim their condemnation from our
severer judgment.

It is remarkable that those whom the world
least accuses, accuse themselves the most ; and
that a foolish speech, which at the time of
its utterance was unobserved as such by all
who heard it, shall yet remain fixed in the
memory of him who pronounced it, with a
tenacity which he vainly seeks to communicate
to more agreeable subjects of reflection.   It is
also remarkable that whilst our own foibles,
or our imagined exposure of them to others,
furnish the most frequent subject of almost
nightly regret, yet we rarely recall to recollection our acts of consideration for the feelings
of others, or those of kindness and benevolence.
These are not the familiar friends of our
memory, ready at all times to enter the domi-
cile of mind its unbidden but welcome guests.
When they appear, they are usually summoned
at the command of reason, from some un-

expected ingratitude, or when the mind retires
within its council chamber to nerve itself for
the endurance or the resistance of injustice.

If such be the pain, the penalty of thought-
less folly, who shall describe the punishment
of real guilt ?   Make but the offender better,
and he is already severely punished.   Memory,
that treacherous friend but faithful monitor,
recalls the existence of the past, to a mind
now imbued with finer feelings, with sterner
notions of justice than when it enacted the
deeds thus punished by their recollection.

If additional knowledge be given to us, the
consequences of many of our actions appear in
a very altered light.   We become acquainted
with many evils they have produced, which, although quite unintentional on our part, are yet
a subject of painful regret.   But this unavailing
regret is mixed with another feeling far more
distressing.   We reproach ourselves with not
having sufficiently employed the faculties we

L

possessed in acquiring that knowledge, which, if we had attained, would have prevented us from committing acts we now discover to have been injurious to those we best loved.

On the other hand, the good which such increased knowledge enables us to discover that we have *unintentionally* done, fails to pro-duce that satisfaction always arising from a vir-tuous motive ; and it is accompanied by the regret that, by a sufficient cultivation of our faculties, we might have enjoyed a still higher satisfaction, by a more efficient service to our fellow-creatures.

Thus, on whichsoever side we look at the question, knowledge *alone* is advantageous to virtue; and if additional knowledge *alone* were given in a future life, it would cause the best of us to regret the errors of the present.

Let us now consider the consequences of a higher tone of moral feeling—of a perception

of excellencies of character, hitherto unap-
preciated.

Without the torment arising from additional
knowledge, we may, in such circumstances,
perceive, that the pain we have inflicted for
imagined offences was quite beyond their real
deserts; and we may feel that the justice we
have done to others, has been quite dispropor-
tioned to the sacrifices they have made to
serve us.

If, without any addition to our intellectual
faculties, increased perfection were given to
our bodily senses, the same result would ensue.
Wollaston has shown, that there are sounds of
such a nature, that they can be heard by some
individuals, but are inaudible to others,—a circumstance which may arise either from the
incapacity of the parts of the ear to vibrate in
the same time as those which produced the
sound, or from the force of the sounding body
being insufficient to communicate through the

air motion to those portions of the ear required
for the production of the sensation of hearing.

If we imagine the soul in an after stage of our
existence, connected with a bodily organ of
hearing so sensitive, as to vibrate with motions
of the air, even of infinitesimal force, and if it
be still within the precincts of its ancient abode,
all the accumulated words pronounced from
the creation of mankind, will fall at once on
that ear.   Imagine, in addition, a power of
directing the attention of that organ entirely
to any one class of those vibrations : then will
the apparent confusion vanish at once ; and
the punished offender may hear still vibrating
on his ear the very words uttered, perhaps,
thousands of centuries before, which at once
caused and registered his own condemnation.

It seems, then, that with improved faculties
or increased knowledge, we could scarcely
look back with any satisfaction on our past lives
—that, to the major part of our race, oblivion

would be the greatest boon.   If, however, in a
future state, we could turn from the contem-
plation of our own imperfections, and with increased knowledge apply our minds to the
discovery of nature's laws, and to the invention
of new methods by which our faculties might
be aided in that research, pleasure the most
unalloyed would await us at every stage of
our progress.

Unclogged by the dull corporeal load of matter which tyrannizes even over our most intellectual moments, and chains the ardent spirit
to its unkindred clay, we should advance in the
pursuit, stimulated instead of wearied by our
past exertions, and encountering each new difficulty in the inquiry, with the accumulated
power derived from the experience of the past,
and the irresistible efforts resulting from the
confidence of ultimate success.

Whether, then, we regard our future prospects as connected with a far higher acuteness of

our present senses—or, as purified by more exalted moral feelings—or, as guided by intellectual power, surpassing all we contemplate on earth, we equally arrive at the conclusion, that the mere employment of such enlarged faculties, in surveying our past existence, will be an ample punishment for all our errors; whilst, on the other hand, if that Being who assigned to us those faculties, should turn their application from the survey of the past, to the inquiry into the present and to the search into the future, the most enduring happiness will arise from the most inexhaustible source.

CHAP. XIII.

REFLECTIONS ON FREE WILL.

THE great question of the incompatibility of one of the attributes of the Creator—that of fore-knowledge, with the existence of the free exercise of their will in the beings he has created,—has long baffled human comprehension ; nor is it the object of this chapter to enter upon that difficult question.

As, however, some of the properties of the Calculating Engine seem, although but very remotely, to bear on a similar question, with respect to finite beings, it may, perhaps, not be entirely useless to state them.

It has already been observed, that it is possible so to adjust the engine, that it shall change the law it is calculating into another law at any distant period that may be assigned.

Now, by a similar adjustment, this change may be made to take place at a time not foreseen by the person employing the engine. For example : when calculating a table of squares, it may be made to change into a table of cubes, the first time the square number ends in the figures—

$$269696 ;$$

an event which only occurs at the 99736th calculation ; and whether that fact is known to the person who adjusts the machine or not, is immaterial to the result.

But the very condition on which the change depends, may be impossible. Thus, the change of the law from that of squares to that of cubes may be made to take place the first time the square number ends with a 7. But it is known, that no square number can end in a 7 ; consequently the event, on the happening of which the change is determined, can itself never take place. Yet, the engine retains impressed on it a law, which would be called into action if the event on which it depends could occur in the course of the law it is calculating.

Nay, further, if the observer of the engine is informed, that at certain times he can move the last figure the engine has calculated, and change it into any other, in consequence of which it becomes possible that some future term may end in 7 ; then, after he has so changed the last figure, whenever that terminal figure arrives, all future numbers calculated by the machine will follow the law of the cubes.

— — — — — —
— — — — — —
— — — — — —

—   —   —   —   —   —

—   —   —   —   —   —

—   —   —   —   —   —

—   —   —   —   —   —

—   —   —   —   —   —

These contingent changes may be limited to single exceptions, and the arrival of such exception may be made contingent on a change which is only possible at certain rare periods. For example: the engine may be set to calculate square numbers, and after a certain number of calculations—ten million and fifty-three, for example, it shall be possible to add unity to a wheel in another part of the engine, which in every other instance is immovable. This fact being communicated to the observer, he may either make that addition or refrain from it : if he refrain, the law of the squares will continue for ever ; if he make the addition, one single cube will be substituted for that square number, which ought to occur ten million and five terms beyond the point at which he made the addition ; and after that no future addition will ever become possible, and no future deviation from the law of the squares will ever occur.

CHAP. XIV.

THOUGHTS ON THE ORIGIN OF EVIL.

I had intended to have put into writing the substance of an interesting discussion I once had with a distinguished Philosopher, now no more, but other demands on my time have prevented the completion of this intention.

— — — — — —

— — — — — —

— — — — — —

— — — — — —

CONCLUSION

READER, I have now fulfilled the task I undertook. Labouring under that imputed mental incapacity which the science I cultivate has been stated to produce, I have brought from the recesses of that science the reasonings and illustrations by which I have endeavoured faintly to embody the human conception of the Almighty mind. It is for you to determine whether the trains of thought I have excited have lowered or exalted your previous notions of the power and the knowledge of the Creator.

That prejudice which I have endeavoured to
expose is not a merely speculative opinion, it
is a practical evil; and those whose writings have
been supposed to give support to it, will, I am
sure, feel grieved when they learn that it is
used by the ignorant and the designing, for the
injury of the virtuous and the instructed; that
it is employed as a firebrand, to disturb the relations of social life. They will also, if the
arguments I have used have the same weight
on their minds which they have had on my
own, lament still more deeply that they should
have contributed, in any degree, to throw
discredit on that species of knowledge which
is now found to supply some of the strongest
arguments in favour of religion. I will, however, hope that the opinions I have combated are not shared or even countenanced
by the higher authorities of our Protestant
Church; and I cannot better conclude this
Fragment, than by recalling to the reader the
words of one, whose power of reasoning, and
whose love of truth, add dignity to the high
station he so deservedly fills :—

" Lastly, As we must not dare to withhold
" or disguise revealed *religious* truth, so, we
" must dread the progress of no *other* truth.
" We must not imitate the bigoted Romanists
" who imprisoned Galileo ; and step forward
" Bible in hand (like the profane Israelites car-
" rying the Ark of God into the field of battle)
" to check the inquiries of the Geologist, the
" Astronomer, or the Political-economist, from
" an apprehension that the cause of religion
" can be endangered by them.*   Any theory
" on whatever subject, that is really sound, can
" never be inimical to a religion founded on
" truth ; and any that is unsound may be re-
" futed by arguments drawn from observation
" and experiment, without calling in the aid of
" revelation.   If we give way to a dread of
" danger from the inculcation of any scriptural
" doctrine, or from the progress of physical or
" moral science, we manifest a want of faith in
" God's power, or in his will, to maintain his

* See First Lecture on Political Economy.

" own cause. That we shall indeed best fur-
" ther his cause by fearless perseverance in an
" open and straight course, I am firmly per-
" suaded; but it is not only when we *perceive*
" the mischiefs of falsehood and disguise, and
" the beneficial tendency of fairness and can-
" dour, that we are to be followers of truth :
" the trial of our faith is, when we *cannot* per-
" ceive this : and the part of a lover of truth
" is to follow her at all seeming hazards, after
" the example of Him who ' came into the
" world that He might bear witness to the
" Truth.' "*

* Sermons by the Archbishop of Dublin.

APPENDIX.

APPENDIX.

NOTE A.

ON THE GREAT LAW WHICH REGULATES MATTER.

EVER since the period when Newton established the great law of gravity, philosophers have occasionally speculated on the existence of some more comprehensive law, of which gravity itself is the consequence. Although some have considered it vain to search for a more general law, the great philosopher himself left encouragement to future inquirers; and the time, perhaps, has even now arrived, when such a discovery may be near its maturity. It would occupy too much space to introduce many illustrations of this opinion; there is, however, one which deserves attention, because it is not merely a happy conjecture, but the hypothesis on which it rests has been carried by its author, through the aid of profound mathematical reasoning, to many of its remote consequences.

M 2

M. Mosotti* has shown, that by supposing matter
to consist of two sorts of particles, each of which repels
similar particles, directly as the mass, and inversely as
the squares, of their distances; whilst each attracts those
of the other kind, also according to the same law,—
then the resulting attractions explain all the phenomena of electricity, and there remains a residual force,
acting at all sensible distances, according to the law of
gravity.

Many of the discoveries of the present day point
towards a more general law; and many of the philosophers of the present time anticipate its near approach.
Under these circumstances, it may be interesting as
well as useful briefly to state the principles which such
a law *must* comprehend; and to indicate, however imperfectly, the path to be pursued in the research.

If matter be supposed to consist of two sorts of
particles, or rather, perhaps, of two sorts of centres of
force, of different orders of density; and if the particles of each order repel their own particles, according
to a given law, but attract particles of the other kind,
according to another law,—then, if we conceive only
one particle of the denser kind to exist, and an infinite

* Professor of Physics at the University of the Ionian Islands.—
The paper of M. Mosotti has been translated, and published by Mr.
R. Taylor, in the third number of the Scientific Memoirs; a work
which it is proposed shall contain translations of all the most important
original papers printed in foreign countries.

number of the other kind, that single particle will become the centre of a system, surrounded by all the others, which will form around it an atmosphere denser near the central body.

If we conceive a stream of particles, similar to those forming the atmosphere, to impinge upon it, so as just to overcome its resistance, they will, whilst continually producing undulations throughout its whole extent, gradually increase its magnitude, until it attains such a size, that the repulsion of the particles at its outer surface is just balanced by the attraction of the central particle. If the stream continue after this point is reached, the whole outer layer will be pressed a little beyond the limit of attraction, and will fly off at right angles to the surface, which might then be said to radiate.

If the whole of the space in which such a central particle with its atmosphere is placed, is itself full of atmospheric particles, then their density will increase in approaching the central body; and if a stream of such particles were directed towards the centre, they might produce throughout the atmosphere vibrations, which would be transmitted from it in all directions.

If two such central particles, with their atmospheres, exist at a distance from each other, they will be drawn together by a force depending on the *difference* between the mutual repulsion of their atmospheres and central bodies respectively for each other, and the attraction of each central particle for its neighbour's atmosphere : and in order to coincide with the existing law of nature, this must be directly as the mass, and inversely as the square, of the distance. The other conditions which such a law must satisfy, are—

1. That the juxtaposition of such atoms must, in some circumstances, form a solid body.

2. In other circumstances, a fluid.

3. That again, in still other circumstances, its particles shall repel each other, or the body become gaseous.

4. In the first state the body must possess cohesion, tenacity, malleability, elasticity ; the measure and extent of each of which must result generally from the original law, and in each particular case from the constants belonging to the substance itself.

5. In the second, it must possess capillarity, susceptibility of being compressed without becoming solid, as also elasticity.

But besides these, the *central* atoms must admit of a more intimate approach, so that their atmospheres may unite and form one atmosphere. This might constitute chemical union. Binary compounds might then (supposing the distance between the two central particles to be very small, compared with the diameters of the atmospheres) have atmospheres not quite spherical, and attracting differently in different directions; thus possessing polarity. Combinations of three or more atoms, as the central body of one atmosphere, might give great varieties of attractive forces. Each different combination would give a different atmosphere; and the equation of its surface might, perhaps, become the mathematical expression of the substance it constituted. Thus, all the phenomena produced by bodies, acting chemically on each other, might be deduced from the comparison of the *characteristic* surfaces of the atmospheres of their atoms. Another result, also, might ensue. Two or more central atoms uniting, might either not be able to retain the same amount of atmosphere, or they might possibly be able to retain a larger quantity. If the particles of such atmospheres constituted heat, it would in the former case be given out, and in the latter absorbed by chemical union.

Hence the whole of chemistry, and with it crystallography, would become a branch of mathematical analysis, which, like astronomy, taking its constants from observation, would enable us to predict the character of any new compound, and possibly indicate the source from which its formation might be anticipated.

For the sake of simplicity, two species of particles
only have been mentioned above; but it seems more
probable, that matter consists of at least three kinds.

Suppose each kind to repel its own particles; and
supposing the central atom, whilst it repels similar
particles, to attract those of the two other kinds; and
moreover, that these latter were either repulsive, or
indifferent to each other. We might then conceive
matter to be made up of particles, each having a central
point, with an atmosphere surrounding it, and this atmosphere again inclosed within another and larger one.

Under such circumstances, the outer atmosphere
might give rise to heat and light, to solidity and fluidity,
and the gaseous condition; to capillarity, to elasticity,
tenacity, and malleability. The more intimate union
of the central atoms, by which two or more become
enclosed in one common atmosphere of the second
kind, might represent chemical combinations, and perhaps that atmosphere itself be electricity. Possibly,
also, this intermediate atmosphere, acted on by the
pressure of the external one, and by the attraction of
the central atom, might take the liquid form. These
binary or multiple-combinations of the original atoms,
and their smaller atmospheres, would still be enclosed
in an atmosphere of the outer kind, which might be
nearly spherical. The joint action of the three might,
at sensible distances, produce gravity.

The reader should, however, bear in mind, that these hints are but thrown out as objects of reflection and inquiry; and that nothing but a profound mathematical investigation can establish them, or even give to them that temporary value which arises from any hypothesis, representing a large collection of facts.

NOTE B.

ON THE CALCULATING ENGINE.

THE nature of the arguments advanced in this volume having obliged me to refer, more frequently than I should have chosen, to the Calculating Engine, it becomes necessary to give the reader some brief account of its progress and present state.

About the year 1821, I undertook to superintend, for the Government, the construction of an engine for calculating and printing mathematical and astronomical tables. Early in the year 1833, a small portion of the machine was put together, and it performed its work with all the precision which had been anticipated. At that period circumstances, which I could not control, caused what I then considered a temporary suspension of its progress; and the Government, on whose decision the continuance or discontinuance of the work depended, have not yet communicated to me their wishes on the question. The first illustration I have employed is derived from the calculations made by this engine.

About October, 1834, I commenced the design of another, and far more powerful engine. Many of the contrivances necessary for its performance have since been discussed and drawn according to various principles; and all of them have been invented in more than one form. I consider them, even in their present state, as susceptible of practical execution; but time, thought, and expense, will probably improve them. As the remaining illustrations are all drawn from the powers of this new engine, it may be right to state, that it will calculate the numerical value of any algebraical function—that, at any period previously fixed upon, or contingent on certain events, it will cease to tabulate that algebraic function, and commence the calculation of a different one, and that these changes may be repeated to any extent.

The former engine could employ about 120 figures in its calculations; the present is intended to compute with about 4,000.

Here I should willingly have left the subject; but the public having erroneously imagined, that the sums

of money paid to the workmen for the construction of
the engine, were the remuneration of my own services,
for inventing and directing its progress; and a Com-
mittee of the House of Commons having incidentally
led the public to believe that a sum of money was voted
to me for that purpose, I think it right to give to that
report the most direct and unequivocal contradiction.

NOTE C.

EXTRACT FROM THE THEORY OF PROBABILITIES OF LAPLACE.

" Nous devons donc envisager l'état présent de l'univers, comme l'effet de son état antérieur, et comme la cause de celui qui va suivre.

" Une intelligence qui pour un instant donnée, connaîtrait toutes les forces dont la nature est animée, et la situation respective des êtres qui la composent, si d'ailleurs elle était assez vaste pour soumettre ces données à l'analyse, embrasserait, dans la même formule, les mouvemens des plus grands corps de l'univers et ceux du plus léger atome : rien ne serait incertain pour elle, et l'avenir, comme le passé, serait présent a ses yeux. L esprit humain offre, dans la perfection qu'il a su donner à l'astronomie, une faible esquisse de cette intelli-

gence.   Ses découvertes en mécanique et en géométrie,
jointes à celle de la pesanteur universelle, l'ont mis à
portée de comprendre dans les mêmes expressions ana-
lytiques, les états passés et futurs du système du
monde.

" En appliquant le même méthode à quelques autres
objets de ses connaissances, il est parvenu à ramener
à des lois générales, les phénomènes observés, et à
prévoir ceux que des circonstances données doivent
faire éclore.   Tous ses efforts dans la recherche de la
vérité, tendent à le rapprocher sans cesse l'intelligence
que nous venons de concevoir, mais dont il restera
toujours infiniment éloigné.   Cette tendance propre à
l'espèce humaine, est ce qui la rend supérieure aux
animaux ; et ses progrès en ce genre, distinguent les
nations et les siècles, et fondent leur véritable gloire."—
Laplace, Théorie Analytique des Probabilités.

NOTE D.

NOTE TO CHAP. VIII. ON MIRACLES.

THE view taken of miracles in Chapter VIII. is the same as that contained in the work of Butler, on the Analogy of Religion to the Constitution and Course of Nature. Inquiries connected with the Calculating Engine, impressed it very forcibly on my own mind, and I have drawn the illustrations chiefly from that subject. I cannot, however, forbear referring the reader to the opinion of Sir J. Herschel, expressed at the beginning of his letter to Mr. Lyell, (see Note I.) because it confirms me in the belief, that the more profoundly we inquire into the mechanism of nature, the more certainly we arrive at that conclusion.

NOTE E.

NOTE TO CHAPTER X. ON HUME'S ARGUMENT AGAINST MIRACLES.

THE example in the text is sufficient to show that the conclusion at which Hume arrived respecting the sufficiency of testimony to support a miracle, will not bear the test of a numerical examination. It may, however, be interesting to point out the amount of testimony required, under different circumstances.

The reader will observe, that throughout the chapter to which this note refers, as well as in the note itself, the argument of Hume is taken strictly according to his own interpretation of the terms he uses, and the calculations are founded on them; so that it is from the very argument itself, when fairly pursued to its full extent, that the refutation results.

Both our belief in the truth of human testimony, and our belief in the permanence of the laws of nature, are, according to Hume, founded on experience; we may, therefore, in the complete ignorance in which he assumes we are, with respect to the causes of either, treat the question as one of the probability of an event deduced solely from observations of the past.

If an event has been observed to happen m times in succession, it is known that the probability of its happening the next time is $\frac{m+1}{m+2}$, and the probability of its not arriving is $\frac{1}{m+2}$.* If we suppose m to represent the amount of the uniform experience of all mankind, from the creation to the present time, it will be a very large number, and $\frac{1}{m+2}$ will represent the probability of the occurrence of a miracle opposed to that experience.

Again: if it is found from experience, that a certain class of men out of every p statements, make one of them false, either from ignorance or design, then the

* "On trouve ainsi qu'un évènement étant arrivé de suite, un nombre quelconque de fois; la probabilité qu'il arrivera encore la fois suivante est égale à ce nombre augmenté de l'unité, divisé par le même nombre augmenté de deux unités."—*Laplace's Théorie Analytique des Probabilités*, p. xiii.

N

probability of the falsehood of a statement made by such a person, is $\dfrac{1}{p}$.

The probability that two such persons will concur in falsehood, is $\dfrac{1}{p^2}$;

and the probability of the concurrence of n such persons in an error, is $\dfrac{1}{p^n}$.

Now, according to Hume's argument, the *falsehood* of the testimony by which a miracle is supported, must be a *more miraculous* event than the *occurrence of the miracle* itself.

Here, then, we have for the measure of the improbability of the testimony $\dfrac{1}{p^n}$, and for that of the occurrence of the miracle $\dfrac{1}{m+2}$; and, in order to prove the miracle, the first improbability must be greater than the second. But this can only happen when

$$p^n > m + 2.$$

Hence, $n \log. p > \log. (m+2)$

and $n > \dfrac{\log. (m+2)}{\log. p}$.

It follows, therefore, that however large m may be, or however great the quantity of experience against the occurrence of a miracle, (provided only that there are persons whose statements are more frequently correct than incorrect, and who give their testimony in favour of it without collusion,) a certain number n can ALWAYS be found; so that *it shall be a greater improbability that they shall agree in error, than that the miracle shall occur.*

Let us suppose each of the witnesses who gives independent testimony, makes one erroneous statement in ten; then

$$n > \frac{\log. (m + 2)}{\log. 10} > \log. (m + 2).$$

And, moreover, let us suppose the number of places of figures contained in $m + 2$, to be k; then $\log. (m + 2)$ is nearly equal to $k - 1$, and

$$n > k - 1.$$

Now let the number of observed instances in which the miracle has not occurred be a million million;

or, 1,000,000,000,000,

then the number of such witnesses necessary to prove its occurrence is

$$n > \log. (10^{12} + 2) > 12,$$

or thirteen such witnesses are sufficient.

If $p = 100$, then we must have for the number of such witnesses,

N 2

$$n > \frac{\log.\,(m + 2)}{\log.\,100} > \frac{\log.\,(m + 2)}{2} \; ;$$

and if, as before, m is a million millions,

$$n > \frac{\log.\,(10^{12} + 2)}{2} > \frac{12}{2} > 6,$$

or seven witnesses, are sufficient.

It may be proper to remark, that if a person has established his power to work a miracle in one or more instances, the probability of his being able to do so in any other case becomes considerable, whatever may be the probability of his usual statements. For, as we have observed that in the one or more instances in which he stated that he should perform a miracle, the event followed his prediction; and, also, that in no instance it failed to follow such prediction: we must treat the case in the same manner as the occurrence of an event m times in succession; and, if he have performed m miracles, the probability that he will perform any other which he predicts is $\dfrac{m + 1}{m + 2}$;

or, if he has performed a miracle only once, it is two to one that he has power to perform the next miracle he predicts.

The view explained in the chapter of the text to which this note refers, was taken previously to my perusal of the observations of Dr. Chalmers " on the

power which lies in the concurrence of distinct testi-
monies,"* contained in a work pointed out to me by
a friend to whom I had mentioned the subject. Dr.
Chalmers' view is, I believe, substantially the same as
my own, as far as relates to the effect of concurrent
testimony; and had the nature of his work admitted
the introduction of algebraic operations, he would,
most probably, have combined it with the other
principle I have employed, of the probability of the
occurrence of a future event from observations of the
past, and thus have arrived at the complete answer to
the argument of Hume against miracles, by not only
showing the possibility of supporting them by testimony, but even of ascertaining, in any given circumstances, the precise number of witnesses required.

* Evidences of the Christian Revelation, vol i. p. 129.

NOTE F.

ON THE CONSEQUENCES OF CENTRAL HEAT.

THE increase of temperature observed as we descend below the earth's surface, as well as other phenomena, have led to a very general opinion, that great heat exists in the interior of the earth, and that the body of our planet, having been at one time intensely heated, has cooled down to its present temperature. With the view of pointing out courses of inquiry, by which these opinions may ultimately be tested by observation, it is expedient to take a cursory view of some of the consequences of such an hypothesis.

And first, let us imagine the exterior of our globe to have once been in a state of intense heat. No fluid such as water could then have existed on its surface: it would instantly have been converted into vapour; and notwithstanding the increased weight of atmosphere thus produced, and pressing on its surface, sufficient heat would have reduced all fluids to the gaseous state. Let us, however, inquire as to the possible extent of such an atmosphere.

In the first place, it could not extend beyond that point at which the moon's attraction is equal to that of the earth. In the next place, much more contracted limits would be prescribed by the effect of centrifugal force, and of the cooling of the vapour by expansion, and by its distance from the source of radiant heat, which had produced that state.

It would be interesting to inquire, what would be the nature of the surface of the atmosphere under such circumstances. At the distance at which the centrifugal force is equal to that of gravity, it might happen that the temperature was scarcely sufficient to maintain the water in a gaseous state. Should this have been the case, a belt of perpetual clouds might have been formed, resembling those of Jupiter.

If, at this limit, a still lower degree of temperature prevailed, instead of a belt of clouds, a ring of ice might be formed.

This ring of ice, being exposed to different effects of radiation from various parts of the earth's surface,

might, by the superior heat at one part, become diminished, whilst the condensation of vapours might
augment less exposed parts: and these conditions
might continue, until at last the ring itself was melted
through at one point, and the whole would fall down
on the surface of the planet. The tearing up of that
surface from such an event, would be augmented by
the sudden conversion of the solid ice into steam; and
after a time, the fragments of the ring would be absorbed again into the atmosphere of the planet.

Let us now suppose, owing to the gradual cooling
down of the whole globe, the limit of condensation of
steam into water, to occur at a nearer point than that at
which the centrifugal force equals that of gravity. As
soon as the steam is condensed into water, it will descend towards the surface of the earth; but that surface
being still very hot, will, by its radiation, again convert the descending shower into steam; and this will
happen at different heights above the surface, according to the radiating power of the part below. We
may, therefore, conceive a shell surrounding the earth,
the outer surface of which has just been condensed into
water, and the inner consists of vapour, just re-con-
verted into that state by the earth's radiation. These
surfaces will attain different heights in different places.
Between these two surfaces there will exist a perpetual
rain, descending from the upper as a gentle shower,
becoming gradually a violent current, and then as

it falls re-absorbed into another gentle shower, which is entirely absorbed in approaching the heated surface.

Such being the state of things, let us imagine the globe to cool down uniformly. The lower surface of the descending rain, which is placed at irregular heights, will at length be brought down to the earth's surface in one or more points. The effect of this, which will in the first instance be a gentle shower, would be to cool that portion of the surface on which it falls, and hence to diminish its radiating power. This change, in its turn, will lower the under surface of the watery shell, so that a more violent rain, and ultimately an impetuous torrent will continue, perhaps, for thousands of years, its unintermitted vertical action on the surface exposed to its force. The excavation of the largest valleys, or even of ocean beds, is not too much to expect from such forces.

But let us take another view of the consequences of such an original state of incandescence. The whole of the fluids now on the surface of the earth must then have been suspended in its atmosphere. But the extent of that atmosphere is itself limited by various causes: the attraction of other bodies, the effects of centrifugal force, the decrease of temperature, and the distances at which the particles of gaseous bodies cease to repel each other, all have their influence in determining its form and magnitude. Let us suppose that we possessed data from which the approximate amount

of vapour contained in the entire atmosphere were
known, and consequently the whole amount of water
in it; then, since we know the area of the present seas,
we might easily ascertain their average depth. If the
result of such a computation should give a mean depth
much less than that which we know the ocean to possess,—as, for instance, only a hundred feet,—then we
might conclude, either that the surface of the earth had
never been in such a state of incandescence as has been
supposed, or that if it had, that a new source of aqueous
vapour had been supplied to it, subsequently to its
cooling down.

NOTE G.

ON THE ACTION OF EXISTING CAUSES IN PRODUCING ELEVATIONS AND SUBSIDENCES IN PORTIONS OF THE EARTH'S SURFACE.

THE following explanation of the origin of many of the changes at present going on on the earth's surface, was suggested in endeavouring to account for the very singular phenomena presented by the temple of Jupiter Serapis, at Puzzuoli, near Naples. The facts relating to that temple were stated in a paper presented to the Geological Society of London, in March, 1834; an abstract of which was published shortly after.

The following positions are taken as the basis of the reasoning on this subject:—

1. That, as we descend below the surface of the earth, the temperature increases.

2. That solid rocks expand by being heated; but
that clay, and some other substances, contract under
the same circumstances.

3. That different rocks and strata conduct heat
differently.

4. That the earth radiates heat differently, at different parts of its surface, according as it is covered
with forests, with mountains, with deserts, or with water.

5. That existing atmospheric agents, and other
causes, are constantly changing the condition of the
surface of the globe.

The only one of these propositions on which, in the
present state of knowledge, the slightest question can be
raised, is the first. But the observations on which it
depends have latterly become so numerous, that the
general fact of an increase of temperature, on descending into the crust of the earth, can scarcely be ques-
tioned; although the exact law of this increase, and
the extent to which it penetrates, are yet undecided.

An increase of 1° Fahrenheit's thermometer, for every
50 or 60 feet we penetrate below the earth's surface,
seems nearly the average result of observations. If the
rate continue, it is obvious that, at a small distance below
the earth's surface, we shall arrive at a heat which will

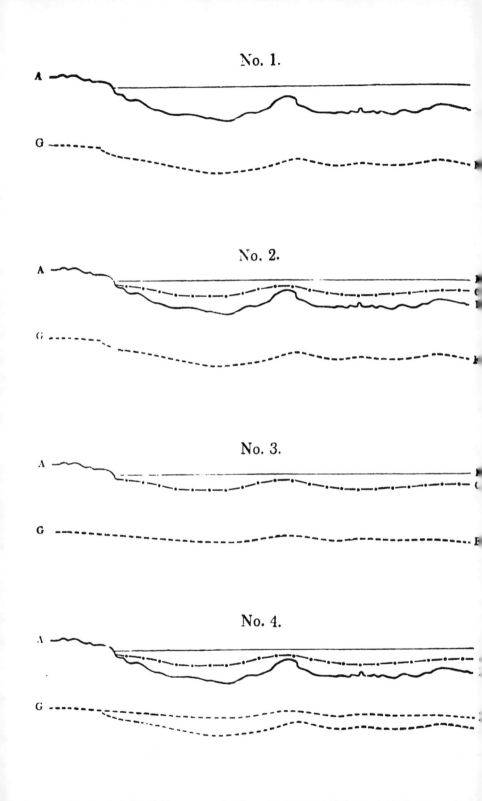

No. 1.

A

G

No. 2.

A

G

No. 3.

A

G

No. 4.

A

G

keep all substances with which we are acquainted in a state of fusion. Without, however, assuming the fluidity of the central nucleus,—a question yet unsettled, and which rests on very inferior evidence* to that by which the principles here employed are supported,—we may yet arrive at important conclusions ; and these may be applied to the case of central fluidity, according to the opinions of the inquirer.

If we consider the temperature of any point:—for example, G, situated two miles below the surface of an elevated table land, A, in the annexed wood-cut; and if we imagine a surface passing through all the points of equal temperature ; then, as this surface passes under the adjacent ocean, which we may suppose, on an average, to be two miles deep, it is evident that the *surface of equal heat* will descend towards the earth's centre ; because, if it did not, we should have great heat nearly in contact with the bottom of the sea. In the first figure, B is the surface of the ocean. A D, the surface of the land, and of the bed of the ocean. The broken line, G F, is the isothermal line. Let us now suppose, by the continual wearing down of the continents and islands adjoining this ocean, that it becomes nearly filled up. The broken line C, in the second figure of the wood-cut, indicates the new bottom. The

* The reader will find this question fully discussed in the 17th chapter of Lyell's Geology ; On the Causes of Earthquakes and Volcanos.

former bottom of the ocean being now covered with a
bad conductor of heat, instead of with a fluid which
rapidly conveyed it away, the surface of uniform temperature will rise, slowly but considerably, as is shown
at G E, in the third figure. In the fourth figure, the
first bed of the ocean, A D, and its isothermal line,
G F, as well as the new bed, A C, of the ocean, and its
corresponding isothermal line, G E, are all shown at
one view.

The newly formed strata will be consolidated by
the application of heat; they may, perhaps, contract
in bulk, and thus give space for new deposits, which
will, in their turn, become similarly consolidated.
But the surface of uniform temperature below the
bed of that ocean cannot rise towards the earth's
surface, without an increase in the temperature of all
the beds of various rock on which it rests; and this
increase must take place for a considerable depth.
The consequence of this must be a gradual rise of
the ancient bed of the ocean, and of all the deposits newly formed upon it. The shallowness of
this altered ocean will, by exposing it to greater evapo-
ration from the effect of the sun's heat, give increased
force to the atmospheric causes still operating, to fill
it up.

Possibly the conducting power of the heated rocks
may be so slow, that its total effect may not take place

for centuries after the sea has given place to dry land; and we can conceive, in such circumstances, the force of the sun's rays acting on the surface, and the increasing heat from below so consolidating that surface, that it may again descend below the level of adjacent seas, even though its first bottom is still subject to the elevatory process. Thus, a series of shallow seas or large lakes might be formed; and these processes might even be repeated several times, before the full effect of the expansion from below had permanently raised the whole newly-formed land above the effects of the adjacent seas.

If the sea were originally much deeper, or, if in particular parts it were much deeper, as, for instance, ten or twenty miles, then such portion might, after the lapse of many ages, acquire a red, or even a melting heat, and the conversion into gases of some of the substances thus operated on, might give rise to earthquakes, or to subterraneous volcanoes.

On the other hand, as the high land gradually wears away, by the removal of a portion of its thickness, and as the cooling down of its surface takes place, its contraction might give rise to enormous rents. If these cracks penetrate to any great reservoirs of melted matter, such as appear to subsist beneath volcanos, then they will be compressed by the contraction, and the melted matter will rise and fill the cracks, which, when cooled down, will become dykes.

If these rents do not reach the reservoir of melted matter, and if there exist in the neighbourhood any volcanic vents connected with it, the contraction of the upper strata may give rise to volcanic eruptions, through those vents, which might be driven by such a force to almost any height. These eruptions may themselves diminish the heat of the beds immediately above the melting cauldron from which they arise; for the conversion of some of the fluid substances into gases, on the removal of the enormous pressure, will rapidly abstract heat from the melted mass.

As the removal of the upper surface of the high land may diminish its resistance to fracture, so the altered pressure arising from the removal of that weight, and its transport to the bottom of the ocean, may determine the exit of the melted matter.

Other consequences might arise from the different fusibility of the various strata deposited in the bed of the ocean. Let us imagine, in the annexed wood cut, the two beds, A and B, to melt at a much lower tem-

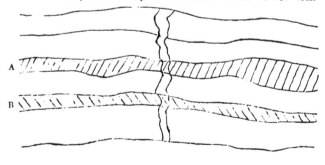

perature than those between which they intervene. It might happen, by the gradual rising of the isothermal surfaces, that one or both of those strata should be melted; and thus, supposing all the beds originally to have contained marine remains, we might, at a distant period, discover two interposed beds, having no trace of animal remains, but presenting all the appearances of former fusion, resting on, separated by, and existing under, other beds of demonstrably marine formation.

If, during that state of fusion, rents should be formed through several of these strata, injection of the liquid matter might proceed both upwards and downwards from these melted beds. If, on the contrary, older dykes had penetrated all these strata, it is possible to suppose such circumstances of fusibility in the older dyke, or of its chemical relation to the melted bed, that the portions passing through that bed shall be obliterated, whilst those portions of the dyke passing through the less fusible beds, protected from such action, shall remain unaltered, as in the annexed cut.

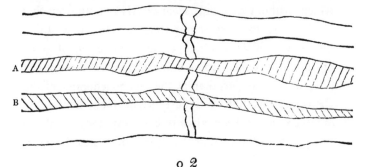

Another consequence of this constant change in the position of the isothermal surfaces must be the development of thermo-electricity, which, acting on an immense scale, may determine the melting of some beds, or the combination of the melted masses of others, or cause the segregation of veins and crystals, in heated, but not fluid, portions of the strata exposed to its influence. Nor may the dykes themselves be without their use, either in keeping up the communication for the passage of electricity, if they are good conductors, or separating the groups of strata which produce it, if they are bad conductors.

For the elucidation of this subject, it appears very important that experiment should be made on the effects of long-continued artificial heat in altering and obliterating the traces of organic remains existing in known rocks. It seems probable that we might, by a well-planned series of such experiments, be able to trace the gradually disappearing structure of animal remains existing in rocks subjected to fire, into marks which, without such aid, seem utterly remote from that origin; and that we might thus establish new alphabets with which to attempt the deciphering of some of the older rocks. Some experiments, with this object in view, were undertaken at the recommendation of the British Association, and portions of rock, containing organic remains, have already been exposed, for above two years, to the heat of the hearth of a blast furnace, at the Elsecar iron works, through the permission of Earl Fitzwilliam, and at the Low Moor works, by that of the proprietors.

It appears, therefore, that in consequence of changes continually going on, by the destruction of forests, the filling up of seas, the wearing down of elevated lands, the heat radiated from the earth's surface varies considerably at different periods.

In consequence of this variation, and also in consequence of the covering up of the bottoms of seas, by the detritus of the land, the *surfaces of equal temperature* within the earth are continually changing their form, and exposing thick beds near the exterior to alterations of temperature. The expansion and contraction of these strata may form rents and veins, produce earthquakes, determine volcanic eruptions, elevate continents, and possibly raise mountain chains.

The consequences resulting from the working out of this theory would fill a' volume, rather than a note. It may, however, be remarked, that whilst the principles on which it is founded are really existing causes, yet that the sufficiency of the theory for explaining all the phenomena can only be admitted when it shall have been shown, that their power is fully equal to produce all the observed effects.

TABLE

Showing the Expansion of Beds of Granite variously heated, from One Degree to One Hundred Degrees Fahrenheit, and from One to Five Hundred Miles thick.

Miles.	One Degree.	Twenty Degrees.	Fifty Degrees.	One Hundred Degrees.
	Feet.	*Feet.*	*Feet.*	*Feet.*
1	·02548	·5095	1·274	2·548
5	·13	2·55	6·37	12·74
10	·25	5·10	12·74	25·48
15	·38	7·64	19·11	38·21
20	·51	10·19	25·48	50·95
25	·64	12·74	31·85	63·69
30	·76	15·29	38·21	76·43
35	·89	17·83	44·58	89·17
40	1·02	20·38	50·95	101·90
45	1·15	22·93	57·32	114·64
50	1·27	25·48	63·69	127·38
55	1·40	28·02	70·06	140·12
60	1·53	30·57	76·43	152·86
65	1·66	33·12	82·80	165·59
70	1·78	35·67	89·17	178·33
75	1·91	38·21	95·5	191·07
80	2·04	40·76	101·90	203·81
85	2·17	43·31	108·27	216·55
90	2·29	45·86	114·64	229·28
95	2·42	48·40	121·01	242·02
100	2·55	50·95	127·38	254·76
150	3·82	76·43	191·07	382·14
200	5·10	101·90	254·76	509·52
500	12·74	254·76	636·90	1273·80

TABLE

*Showing the Expansion of Beds of Granite variously heated,
from Two Hundred Degrees to Three Thousand Degrees
Fahrenheit, and from One to Five Hundred Miles thick.*

Miles.	Two Hundred Degrees.	Five Hundred Degrees.	One Thousand Degrees.	Three Thousand Degrees.
	Feet.	*Feet.*	*Feet.*	*Feet.*
1	5·095	12·738	25·476	76·428
5	25·5	63·7	127·4	382·1
10	51·0	127·4	254·8	764·3
15	76·4	191·1	382·1	1147·4
20	101·9	254·8	509·5	1528·6
25	127·4	318·5	636·9	1910·7
30	152·9	382·1	764·3	2292·8
35	178·3	445·8	891·7	2675·0
40	203·8	509·5	1019·0	3057·1
45	229·3	573·2	1146·4	3439·3
50	254·8	636·9	1273·8	3821·4
55	280·2	700·6	1401·2	4203·5
60	305·7	764·3	1528·6	4585·7
65	331·2	828·0	1655·9	4967·8
70	356·7	891·7	1783·3	5350·0
75	382·1	955·4	1910·7	5732·1
80	407·6	1019·0	2038·1	6114·2
85	433·1	1082·7	2165·5	6496·4
90	458·6	1146·4	2292·8	6878·5
95	484·0	1210·1	2420·2	7260·7
100	509·5	1273·8	2547·6	7642·8
150	764·3	1910·7	3821·4	11464·2
200	1019·0	2547·6	5095·2	15285·6
500	2547·5	6369·0	12738·0	38214·0

The table was calculated from experiments made under the direction of Colonel Totten, by Mr. H. C. Bartlett, of the United States Engineers; an account of which is given in the American Journal of Science, Vol. XXII. p. 136.

From the result of these experiments it was found that, for every degree of Fahrenheit,

Granite expands . . . . ·000004825
Marble . . . . ·000005668
Sandstone . . . . ·000009532

The tables were computed by the Calculating Engine, from the first line, which was deduced from the experiment. It will be observed that the numbers given are always true to the last figure, a compensation which the Engine itself made. In order to find the expansion for marble, increase the numbers by one-sixth. To find the expansion for sandstone, double the numbers found in the table.

Other experiments have since been made by Mr. Adie, of which an account is given in the thirteenth volume of the Transactions of the Royal Society of Edinburgh : from these I have selected the following list of expansions :—

Roman Cement expands . . . . ·00000750
Sicilian White Marble . . . . ·00000613
Carrara Marble . . . . ·00000363

Sandstone, from Craigleith quarry . . . . ·00000652
Slate, from Penrhyn, Wales . . . . ·00000576
Peterhead Red Granite . . . . ·00000498
Arbroath Pavement . . . . ·00000499
Caithness Pavent . . . . ·00000497
Greenstone, from Ratho . . . . ·00000449
Aberdeen Grey Granite . . . . ·00000438
Best Stock Brick . . . . ·00000306
Fire Brick . . . . ·00000274
Black Marble, Galway . . . . ·00000247

NOTE I.

I am happy, through the kindness of Mr. Lyell and Mr. Murchison, to be enabled to put before the reader extracts from some letters of Sir J. Herschel, which show, that though my early friend is extending the boundaries of our system, by his observations in the southern hemisphere, his active and indefatigable mind has yet found time to throw its comprehensive glance over some of the highest questions which perplex other sciences. I feel, that the almost perfect coincidence of his views with my own, gives additional support to the explanations I have offered; whilst the reader will perceive, from the different light in which my friend has viewed the subject, that we were both independently led to the same inferences by different courses of inquiry.

" Fredhausen, Cape of Good Hope, Feb. 20, 1836.

" My dear Sir,

" I am perfectly ashamed not to have long since ac-
" knowledged your present of the new edition of your

" Geology, a work which I now read for the third
" time, and every time with increased interest, as it
" appears to me one of those productions which work
" a complete revolution in their subject, by altering
" entirely the point of view in which it must thence-
" forward be contemplated. You have succeeded, too,
" in adding dignity to a subject already grand, by ex-
" posing to view the immense extent and complication
" of the problems it offers for solution, and by unveiling
" a dim glimpse of a region of speculation connected
" with it, where it seems impossible to venture without
" experiencing some degree of that mysterious awe
" which the sybil appeals to, in the bosom of Æneas,
" on entering the confines of the shades—or what the
" Maid of Avenel suggests to Halbert Glendinning,

' He that on such quest would go must know nor fear nor failing ;
To coward soul or faithless heart the search were unavailing.'

" Of course I allude to that mystery of mysteries, the
" replacement of extinct species by others. Many
" will doubtless think your speculations too bold, but
" it is as well to face the difficulty at once. For my
" own part, I cannot but think it an inadequate con-
" ception of the Creator, to assume it as granted that
" his combinations are exhausted upon any one of the
" theatres of their former exercise, though in this, as
" in all his other works, we are led, by all analogy, to
" suppose that he operates through a series of inter-
" mediate causes, and that in consequence the origina-

" tion of fresh species, could it ever come under our
" cognizance, would be found to be a natural in con-
" tradistinction to a miraculous process—although we
" perceive no indications of any process actually in
" progress which is likely to issue in such a result."

— — — — — —

— — — — — —

— — — — — —

— — — — — —

— — — — — —

" Now for a bit of theory. Has it ever occurred to
" you to speculate on the probable effect of the trans-
" fer of pressure from one part to another of the earth's
" surface by the degradation of existing and the for-
" mation of new continents—on the fluid or semi-fluid
" matter beneath the outer crust? Supposing the
" whole to float on a sea of lava, the effect would
" merely be an almost infinitely minute flexure of the
" strata; but, supposing the layer next below the
" crust to be partly solid and partly fluid, and com-
" posed of a mixture of fixed rock, liquid lava, and
" other masses, in various degrees of viscidity and
" mobility, great inequalities may subsist in the dis-
" tribution of pressure, and the consequence may be,
" local disruptions of the crust, where weakest, and
" escape to the surface of lava, &c.   If the obstructions
" to free communication among distant parts of a fluid

" be great, no *instantaneous* propagation of pressure
" can subsist, the hydrostatical law of the equality of
" pressure being only true of fluids in a state of un-
" disturbed equilibrium. If the whole contents of the
" fissures, pipes, &c., into which we may consider the
" interior divided, were lava, it is true no increase of
" pressure on the bed of an ocean, from deposited
" matter, could force the lava up to a higher level than
" the surface, or so high. But if the contents be
" partly liquid, partly gaseous, or partly water, in a
" state to become steam, at a diminished pressure,
" then it may happen that the joint specific gravity of
" lava + gas, or lava + steam occupying any given chan-
" nel may be less than that of water; or of the joint
" column of water + newly deposited matter—which
" may be brought to press upon it by any sudden giving
" way of support, and the effect will be the escape of
" a mixture of lava and gas, either together, as froth
" and pumice, or by fits, according as they are disposed
" in the channel. This (taken as a general cause of
" volcanos) would account for the great quantity of
" gaseous matter which always accompanies eruptions,
" and for the final *blow out* of wind and dust with
" which they so often terminate. It has always been
" my greatest difficulty in Geology to find a *primum*
" *mobile* for the volcano, taken as a general, not a
" local phenomenon. Davy's speculations about the
" oxidation of the alkaline metals seems to me a mere
" chemical dream, and the fermentation of water and

" pyrites as utterly insignificant on a scale of any
" magnitude. Poulett Scrope's notion of solid rocks
" flashing out into lava and vapour, on *removal of*
" *pressure*, and your statement of the probable cause of
" Volcanic Eruptions, in p. 385, vol. ii. 4th Ed. when
" you speak of the effect of a minute hole bored in a
" tube, in which liquefied gases are imprisoned, both
" appear to me wanting in explicitness, and as not going
" high enough in the inquiry, up to its true beginning,
" and also as giving, in some respects, a wrong notion
" of the process itself. The question stares us in the
" face—How came the gases to be so condensed?
" Why did they submit to be urged into liquefac-
" tion? If they were not originally elastic, but have
" become so by subterranean heat, whence came
" the heat? and *why did it come?* How came the
" pressure to be removed, or what caused the crack?
" &c. &c.

" It seems clear that if the gases, or aqueous vapour,
" were once free, at so high a degree of elasticity as
" is presumed, there exists no adequate cause for their
" confinement,—the spring once uncoiled, there is
" nowhere a power capable of bending it up to the
" pitch. We are forced therefore to admit, that the
" elastic force has been superadded to them, during
" their sojourn below, by an accession of temperature.
" Now, though I cannot agree with you in your view
" of the subject of the Central heat, p. 373, vol. ii. 4th

" Ed. (because I see no reason why the heat may not
" go on increasing *to the very centre* without necessitat-
" ing such disturbance of equilibrium as to give rise to
" any circulation of currents, which you there seem to
" regard as the necessary consequence of such a state*),
" yet I agree entirely with what you observe in p. 376,
" —that the ordinary repose of the surface argues a
" wonderful inertness in the interior, where, in fact,
" I conceive that every thing is motionless. Under
" these circumstances, and debarred from that obvious
" means of boiling our pot, the invasion of a circulat-
" ing current, or casual injection of intensely hot
" liquid matter from below, the question, ' *Whence*
" *comes the heat?*' and ' *Why did it come?*' remains
" to be answered on sound theoretical grounds. Now,
" the answer I conceive to be as follows :—

    " Granting an equilibrium of temperature and pres-
" sure within the globe, the isothermal strata near
" the centre will be spherical, but where they approach
" the surface will, by degrees, conform themselves to
" the configuration of the *solid* portion ; that is, to the
" bottom of the sea and the surface of continents.

---

* " Heated liquids circulate not because the lower parts are *hotter*, but
" because they are *lighter*, than the upper. But in the interior of a
" heated globe, the density depends not only on the temperature, but
" on the *pressure* (i. e. the depth) of each stratum ; so that nothing is
" easier than to imagine a law of increasing temperature which shall
" co-exist with increasing density.

" Suppose such a state of equilibrium, and that under
" the bottom B of my great ocean D E, the isother-
" mal strata are as represented by the black lines.

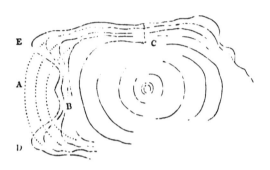

" Now, let that basin be filled with solid matter up to
" A. Immediately the equilibrium of temperature
" will be disturbed. Why?—because the form of a
" stratum of temperature depends essentially on the
" form of the bounding surface of the solid above it,
" that form being one of the arbitrary functions which
" enter into its partial differential equation. Im-
" mediately, therefore, the temperature will begin to
" migrate from below upwards, and the isothermal
" strata will gradually change their forms from the
" black to the dotted lines. The lowest portions at
" B will then (after the lapse of ages, and when a
" fresh state of equilibrium is attained) have acquired
" the temperature of the stratum C, corresponding
" to *their then* actual depth, while a point as deep
" below B as C is below the surface, will have ac-

" quired a much higher temperature, and *may become*
" *actually melted, and that without any bodily transfer*
" *of matter in a liquid state from below.* But if C be
" already at the melting point, B will now be so—
" i. e. the lower level will attain B, and the bottom of
" the new strata will melt, *water included,* with which,
" from the circumstances of the case, they must be
" saturated.

" Now, let the process of deposition go on, until,
" by accumulation of pressure on the bottom or sloping
" sides, or on some protuberance from the bottom,
" some support gives way—a piece of the solid crust
" breaks down, and is plunged into the liquid below,
" and a crack takes place extending upwards. Into
" this the liquid will rise by simple hydrostatic pres-
" sure. But as it gains height, it is less pressed; and
" if it attain such a height that the ignited water can
" become steam, the case before alluded to arises, the
" joint specific gravity of the column is suddenly
" diminished, and up comes a jet of mixed steam and
" lava, till so much has escaped that the deposited
" matter takes a fresh bearing, when the evacuation
" ceases, and the crack becomes sealed up.

" In the analysis I have above given of the process
" of heating from below, we have, if I mistake not, a
" strictly theoretical account of that great desidera-
" tum of the Huttonian theory—' Let heat,' says he,

" ' invade a newly deposited stratum from below.'—
" But why ? Not because great currents of melted
" matter are circulating in the nucleus of the globe—
" not because great waves of caloric are rushing to and
" fro, without a law and without a cause in the subter-
" ranean regions—but simply because the fact of new
" strata *having* been deposited, alters the conditions of
" the equilibrium of temperature, and they draw the
" heat to them, or, which comes to the same thing,
" retain it *in* them in its transit outwards (the supply
" from the centre being supposed inexhaustible, and
" ITS temperature of course invariable).

" According to the general tenor of your book, we
" may conclude, that the greatest transfer of material to
" the bottom of the ocean, is produced at the coast line
" by the action of the sea ; and that the quantity carried
" down by rivers from the surface of continents, is
" comparatively trifling. While, therefore, the greatest
" local accumulation of pressure is in the central area
" of deep seas, the *greatest local relief* takes place along
" the abraded coast lines. Here, then, in this view,
" should occur the chief volcanic vents. If the view
" I have taken of the motionless state of the interior
" of the earth be correct, there appears no reason why
" any such influx of heat should take place under an
" existing continent (say Scandinavia) as to heat incum-
" bent rocks (whose bases retain their level) 5 or 600°
" Fahr. for many miles in thickness. (Princ. of Geol.

" vol. ii. p. 384. 4th Ed.) Laplace's* idea of the elevation
" of surface due to columnar expansion (which you at-
" tribute, in a note, to Babbage,) is in this view in-
" adequate to explain the rise of Scandinavia, or of
" the Andes, &c. But, in the variation of local pres-
" sure due to the transfer of matter by the sea, on the
" bed of an ocean imperfectly and unequally support-
" ed, it seems to me an adequate cause may be found.
" Let A be Scandinavia, B the adjacent ocean (the North
" Sea), C a vast deposit, newly laid on the original bed
" D of the ocean; E E E a semi-fluid, or mixed

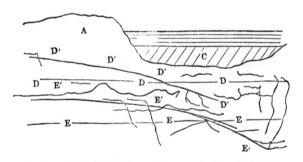

" mass, on which D D D reposes. What will be the
" effect of the enormous weight thus added to the bed
" DDD (rock being heavier than sea)? Of course,

---

* " Nisi Mitscherlich's. I remember well to have read it somewhere
or other."

[This was written before my friend had received the abstract of the
Paper on the Temple of Serapis, forwarded to him by Mr. Lyell. The
reader will perceive, by Note G. of the Appendix, that *isothermal surfaces* form the prominent feature of both our views of this question.—
C. B.]

" to depress D under it, and to force it down into the
" yielding mass E, a portion of which will be driven
" laterally under the continent A, and upheave it.
" Lay a weight on a surface of soft clay : you depress
" it below, and raise it around the weight. If the
" surface of the clay be dry and hard, it will crack in
" the change of figure."

" I don't know whether I have made clear to you
" my notions about the effects of the removal of mat-
" ter from above, to below, the sea. 1st. It produces
" a mechanical subversion of the *equilibrium of pres-*
" *sure.* 2dly. It also, and by a different process (as
" above explained at large), produces a subversion of
" the equilibrium of temperature. The last is the most
" important. *It must be an excessively slow process,*
" and will depend, 1st, on the depth of matter depo-
" sited ; 2dly, on the quantity of water retained by it
" under the great squeeze it has got; 3dly, on the
" tenacity of the incumbent mass—whether the influx
" of caloric from below, WHICH MUST TAKE PLACE,
" acting on that water, shall either heave up the whole
" mass, as a continent, or shall crack *it*, and escape

" as a submarine volcano, or shall be suppressed
" until the mere weight of the continually accumulat-
" ing mass breaks its lateral supports at or near the
" coast lines, and opens there a chain of volcanos.

" Thus the circuit is kept up—the *primum mobile*
" is the degrading power of the sea and rains (both
" originating in the sun's action) above, and the
" inexhaustible supply of heat from the enormous
" reservoirs below, always escaping at the surface, un-
" less when repressed by an addition of fresh clothing,
" at any particular part. In this view of the subject,
" the *tendency is outwards.* Every continent deposited
" has a propensity to rise again ; and the destructive
" principle is continually counterbalanced by a re-or-
" ganizing principle from beneath. Nay, it may go
" farther—there may be such a tendency in the globe
" to swell into froth at its surface, as may maintain its
" dimensions in spite of its expense of heat ; and thus
" preserve the uniformity of its rotation on its axis, in
" spite of the doctrines of refrigeration and contrac-
" tion, (which, by the bye, had occurred to myself,
" and been rejected, as inadequate to give a general
" formula of explanation of volcanos, &c.) Perhaps
" I shall recur to this subject on some future occa-
" sion ; but really the stars leave me very little time
" to lick into form any geological theories, or even
" to examine them with any degree of scrupulous
" severity."

"Feldhausen, Cape of Good Hope, Nov. 15, 1836.

" In the letter you allude to as having been written
" by me to Mr. Lyell, there were some speculations
" about the effect of central heat on newly-deposited
" matter, which, judging from some expressions in his
" answer to that letter, I am inclined to think must
" have been put obscurely, since he appears disposed
" to regard the view I took of the subject as identical
" with some theory ascribed to Mr. Babbage (but, I
" believe, before propounded by Mitscherlich) about
" the elevation of strata by *pyrometric expansion* of the
" subjacent columns of rock, by an invasion of subter-
" raneous heat. *Granting the heat*, there is no difficulty
" in deducing expansions, disruptions, tumefactions,
" &c. ; but *this* was not my drift. Will it be tres-
" passing too much on your patience if I here state, in
" brief, what I really had in view—which, so far as I
" can recollect, has not hitherto been duly, or not at
" all, considered ? If you like to call it my ' theory,'
" you may do so ; but it is not so much ' a theory,' as a
" pursuing into its consequences, according to admitted
" laws, of the hypothesis of a high central tempera-
" ture, which many geologists admit, and all are fa-
" miliar with.

" Granting, then, as a postulate, a gradation of
" temperature within the globe, from the observed ex-
" ternal temperature at the surface, up to a high state

" of incandescence at the centre: I say, that when solid
" matter comes to be deposited to any considerable
" thickness on any part of the bed of the ocean, by sub-
" sidence, (or even on the surface of a continent, by
" volcanic ejection, as in great volcanic plateaux and
" table-lands, or by the action of the wind, as in sand
" hills,) the mere fact of such accession of materials,
" *without requiring any other condition, or concomitant*
" *cause*, will, of itself, in virtue of the known laws of
" the propagation of heat through a slowly-conducting
" mass, immediately subvert the equilibrium of tem-
" perature, and induce a change in the form of the
" isothermal surfaces (curves of equal temperature) in
" the whole region immediately beneath, and surround-
" ing the point of deposition—causing all those surfaces
" (which, you will observe, are only imaginary mathe-
" matical ones, like lines of equal variation in a mag-
" netic chart—not real strata) to bulge outwards, and
" recede from the centre in that part. The direct con-
" sequence of this will be, that any given point of the
" surface on which the deposit took place will, when a
" new state of equilibrium is attained, (supposing it to
" be so) have a temperature corresponding to an iso-
" thermal surface *of a deeper order:* i. e., it will have
" become hotter than it was previous to the new de-
" posit; and the same is true of every point in the
" vertical line drawn from that point downwards. Sup-
" posing, as before said, a new state of equilibrium to
" be attained, (the deposition ceasing, by the filling up

" of the sea in that part) then the temperature of the
" lowest parts of the newly-formed strata will be that
" of a point situated beneath the surface of an old con-
" tinent in the same latitude, at a depth equal to the
" thickness of the deposited matter. The thicker, there-
" fore, the deposit, the hotter will its lower portions
" tend to grow; and, if thick enough, they may grow
" red hot, or *even melt*. In the latter case, their supports
" being also melted or softened, may wholly or partially
" yield, *under the new circumstances of pressure*, to
" which they were originally not adjusted; and the
" phenomena of earthquakes, volcanic explosions, &c.,
" may arrive—while, on the other hand, if no cracks
" occur, and all goes on in quiet, the only consequence
" will be, the obliteration of organic remains, and lines
" of stratification, &c.—the formation of new combina-
" tions of a chemical nature, &c. &c.—in a word, the
" production of Lyell's ' metamorphic' rocks.

" The process described above is precisely that by
" which a man's skin grows warmer in a winter day by
" putting on an additional great coat; the flow of heat
" outwards is obstructed, and the surface of congela-
" tion carried to a distance from his person, by the
" accumulation of heat thereby caused beneath by the
" new covering.

" You see, therefore, that my object is to get at a
" geological '*primum mobile*,' in the nature of a *vera*

" *causa,* and to trace its working in a distinct and in-
" telligible manner.   In future, therefore, instead of
" saying, as heretofore, '*Let heat* from below *invade*
" newly-deposited strata (Heaven knows how or why),
" then they will melt, expand,' &c. &c., we shall
" commence a step higher, and say, ' *Let strata be*
" *deposited.*'   Then, as a necessary consequence, and
" according to known, regular, and calculable laws, heat
" *will* gradually invade them from below and around ;
" and, according to its due degree of intensity at any
" assigned time, will expand, ignite, or melt them,
" as the case may be, &c. &c. &c.; and, I mistake
" greatly, if this be not a considerable reform in our
" geological language.

" According to this view of the matter, there is no-
" thing casual in the formation of Metamorphic Rocks.
" All strata, once buried deep enough, (and due TIME
" allowed!!!) must assume that state,—none can
" escape.   All records of former worlds must ulti-
" mately perish.

" P.S.—If you think it worth while to read the above
" speculation whenever a discussion may arise, natu-
" rally leading to it, at any meeting of the Geological
" Society, (not as a formal communication, for I have
" not time to put it into shape, or work it out in detail,
" but incidentally) you are quite at liberty to do so ;
" and I shall be glad to know your own opinion of it."

NOTE K.

ON THE ELEVATION OF BEACHES BY TIDES.

If the earth were a spheroid of revolution, covered by one uniform ocean, two great tidal waves would follow each other round the globe at a distance of twelve hours.

Suppose several high narrow strips of land were now to encircle the globe, passing through the opposite poles, and dividing the earth's surface into several great unequal oceans, a separate tide would be raised in each. When the tidal wave had reached the farthest shore of one of them, conceive the causes that produce it to cease ; then the wave thus raised would recede to the opposite shore, and continue to oscillate until destroyed by the friction of its bed. But if, instead of ceasing to act, the causes which produced the tide were to reappear at the opposite shore of the ocean, at the very moment when the reflected tide had returned to the place of its origin; then the second tide would act in augmentation of the first, and, if this continued, tides of great height might be produced for ages. The result might be, that the narrow ridge dividing the adjacent oceans would be broken through, and the tidal wave traverse a broader tract than in the former ocean. Let us imagine the new ocean to be just so much broader than the old, that the reflected tide would return to the origin of the tidal movement half a tide later than before: then, instead of two superimposed tides, we should have a tide arising from the subtraction of one from the other. The alterations of the height of the tides on shores so circumstanced, might be very small; and this might again continue for ages: thus causing beaches to be raised at very different elevations, without any real alteration in the level either of the sea or land.

If we consider the superposition of derivative tides, similar effects might be found to result; and it deserves inquiry, whether it may not be possible to account for some remarkable and well-attested phenomena by such means.

The gradual elevation during the past century, of one portion of the Swedish coast above the Baltic, is a recognised fact, and has lately been verified by

Mr. Lyell.* It is not probable, from the form and position of that sea, that two tides should reach it distant
by exactly half the interval of a tide, and thus produce
a very small tide ; nor is it likely that by the gradual
but slow erosion of the longer channel, one tide
should almost imperceptibly advance upon the other :
but it becomes an interesting question to examine whether. in other places, under such peculiar circumstances,
it might not be possible that a series of observations of
the heights of tides at two distant periods, might give
a different position for the mean level of the sea at
places so situated.

If we conceive two tides to meet at any point, one of
which is twelve hours later than the other, the elevation of the waters will arise from the joint influence of
both. Let us suppose, that from the abrasion of the
channel, the later tide arrives each time one-hundredth
of a second earlier than before. After about 3,150
years, the high water of the earlier tide will coincide in
point of time with the low water of the later tide : and
the difference of height between high and low water
will be equal to the difference of the height of the two
tides, instead of to their sum, as it was at the first
epoch.

If, in such circumstances, the two tides were nearly

* See Phil. Trans. 1830.

equal in magnitude, it might happen that on a coast so circumstanced, there would at one time be scarcely any perceptible tide; and yet, 3000 years after, the tide might rise 30 or 40 feet, or even higher; and this would happen without any change of relative height in the land and water during the intervening time. Possibly this view of the effects which may arise, either from the wearing down of channels, or the filling up of seas through which tides pass, may be applied to explain some of the phenomena of raised beaches, which are of frequent occurrence.

Natural philosophers are at present not quite agreed upon the mode of determining the mean level of the ocean. Whether it is to be deduced from the averages between the highest and lowest spring tide, or from the averages of all the intermediate ones, or from the means of the instantaneous heights of the tide at all intervening periods—or by whatever other process, its true level is yet to be ascertained. It may, perhaps, also be useful to suggest that, besides the actual level of the sea at any particular place, it would be also desirable to ascertain whether the time of high water at given epochs is not itself a changeable quantity.

These reflections, however, are only thrown out with the view of exciting discussion on a subject involved at present in great mathematical difficulties, and possessing, at the same time, the highest practical importance.

NOTE L.

ON RIPPLE-MARK.

THE small waves raised on the surface of the water, by the passage of a slight breeze, are called Ripple ; and a series of marks, very similar in appearance, which are sometimes seen at low water on the flat part of a sea-beach formed of fine sand, are called ripple-marks. Such marks occur in various strata, and are regarded as evidence of their having formed beneath the sea. Similar appearances occur when a strong wind drives over the face of a sandy plain.

It appears that two fluids of different specific gravity, the lighter passing over the surface of the former, always concur in the formation of ripple. It seems also, that the lines of ripple-mark are at right angles to the direction of the current which forms them.

If a fluid like air pass over the surface of perfectly quiescent water, in a plain absolutely parallel, it will have no effect; but if it impinge on the surface of that water with the slightest inclination, it will raise a small wave, which will be propagated by undulations to great distances. If the direction of the wind is very nearly parallel to the surface of the water, this first wave, being raised above the general surface, will protect that part of the water immediately beyond it from the full effect of the wind, which will therefore again impinge upon the water at a little distance : and, this concurring with the undulation, will tend to produce another small wave, and thus, again, new waves will be produced. But the under surface of the air itself will also assume the form of waves, and so, on the slightest deviation at any one point from absolute parallelism in the two fluids, their whole surfaces will become covered with ripples.

If one of the fluids be water, and the lower fluid be fine sand, partially supported in water, these marks do not disappear when the cause ceases to act, as they do when formed by air on the surface of water. These are the marks we observe when the tide has receded from a flat, sandy shore.

If, after the formation of ripple-marks at the bottom of a shallow sea, some adjacent river or some current deposit upon them the mud which it holds in suspension, then the former marks will be preserved, and new ripple marks may appear above them. Such is the origin of those marks we observe in various sand-stones, from the most recent down to those of the coal measures.

Dr. Fitton informs me, that he found the sand hills on the south of Etaples (in France) consisting of ripple-marks on a large scale. They are crescent-shaped hillocks, many of which are more than a hundred feet high. The height is greatest in the middle of the crescents, declining towards the points; and the slope on the inner side of the crescent, which is remote from the prevailing direction of the winds, is much more rapid than that on which it strikes.

Mr. Lyell has observed and described this mode of formation of ripple on the dunes of sand near Calais; remarking, that in that case there is an actual lateral transfer; the grains of sand being carried by the wind up the less inclined slope of the ripple, and falling over the steep scarp. I have observed the same fact at Swansea.

A similar explanation seems to present itself as the origin of that form of clouds familiarly known as " a mackarel sky"—a wave-like appearance, which probably arises from the passage of a current of air above or below a thin stratum of clouds. The air, being of nearly the same specific gravity as that of the cloud it acts upon, would produce ripple of larger size than would otherwise occur.

The surface of the sun presents to very good telescopes a certain mottled appearance, which is not exactly ripple, and which it is difficult to convey by description. It may, however, be suggested, that wherever such appearances occur, whether in planetary or in stellar bodies, or in the minuter precincts of the dye-house and the engine-boiler, they indicate the fitness of an inquiry, whether there are not two currents of fluid or semi-fluid matter, one moving with a different velocity over the other, the direction of the motion being at right angles to the lines of waves.

Q

NOTE M.

ON THE AGE OF STRATA, AS INFERRED FROM THE RINGS OF TREES EMBEDDED OF THEM.

THE indelible records of past events which are preserved within the solid substance of our globe, may be in some measure understood without that refined analysis on which their complete knowledge depends. The remains of vegetation, and of animal life, embedded in their coeval rocks, attest the existence of other times ; and as science and the arts advance, we shall be enabled to read the minuter details of their living history. The object of the present note is to suggest to the reader a line of inquiry, by which we may still trace some small portion of the history of the past in the fossil woods which occur in so many of our strata.

It is well known that dicotyledonous trees increase in size by the deposition of an additional layer annually between the wood and the bark, and that a transverse section of such trees presents the appearance of a series of nearly concentric irregular rings, the number of which indicates the age of the tree. The relative thickness of these rings depends on the more or less flourishing state of the plant during the years in which they were formed. Each ring may, in some trees, be observed to be subdivided into others, thus indicating successive periods of the same year during which its vegetation was advanced or checked. These rings are disturbed in certain parts by irregularities resulting from branches; and the year in which each branch first sprung from the parent stock may be ascertained by proper sections.

It has been found by experiment, that even the motion imparted to a tree by the winds has an influence on its growth. Two young trees of equal size and vigour were selected and planted in similar circumstances, except that one was restrained from having any motion in the direction of the meridian, by two strong ropes fixed to it, and connecting it to the ground, at some distance to the north and south. The other tree was by similar means prevented from having any motion in the direction of east and west. After several years, both trees were cut down, and the sections of their stems were found to be oval; but the longer axis of the oval of each was in the direction in which it had been capable of being moved by the winds.

These prominent effects are obvious to our senses;
but every shower that falls, every change of temperature that occurs, and every wind that blows, leaves on
the vegetable world the traces of its passage ; slight,
indeed, and imperceptible, perhaps, to us, but not the
less permanently recorded in the depths of those
woody fabrics.

All these indications of the growth of the living
tree are preserved in the fossil trunk, and with them
also frequently the history of its partial decay. Let
us now examine the use we may make of these details
relative to individual trees, when considering forests
submerged by seas, embedded in peat mosses, or
transformed, as in some of the harder strata, into stone.
Let us imagine, that we possessed sections of the
trunks of a considerable number of trees, such as those
occurring in the bed called the *Dirt-bed,** in the island
of Portland. If we were to select a number of trees
of about the same size, we should probably find many
of them to have been contemporaries. This fact would
be rendered probable if we observed, as we doubtless
should do, on examining the annual rings, that some
of them conspicuous for their size occurred at the same
distances of years in several trees. If, for example, we

* The reader will find an account of these fossil trees, and the strata
in which they occur, in several papers by Dr. Buckland, Mr. De la
Beche, and Dr. Fitton, in the Transactions of the Geological Society
of London, vol. iv. Series 2.

found on several trees a remarkably large annual ring, followed at the distance of seven years by a remarkably thin ring, and this again, after two years, followed by another large ring, we should reasonably infer from these trees, that seven years after a season highly favourable to their growth, there had occurred a season peculiarly unfavourable to them: and that after two more years another very favourable season had happened, and that all the trees so observed had existed at the same period of time. The nature of the season, whether hot or cold, wet or dry, would be known with some degree of probability, from the class of tree under consideration. This kind of evidence, though slight at first, receives additional and great confirmation by the discovery of every new ring which supports it; and, by a considerable concurrence of such observations, the succession of seasons might be in some measure ascertained at remote geological periods.

On examining the shape of the sections of such trees, we might perceive some general tendency towards a uniform inequality in their diameters; and we might perhaps observe that the longer axes of the sections most frequently pointed in one direction. If we knew from the species of tree that it possessed no natural tendency to such an inequality, then we might infer that, during the growth of these trees, they were bent most frequently in one direction; and hence an indication of the prevailing winds at that time. In

order to find from which of the two opposite quarters
these winds came, we might observe the centres of
these sections; and we should *generally* find that the
rings on one side were closer and more compressed
than those on the opposite side. From this we might
infer the most exposed side, or that from which the
wind most frequently blew. Doubtless there would
be many exceptions arising from local circumstances—
some trees might have been sheltered from the direct
course of the wind, and have only been acted upon by an
eddy. Some might have been protected by an adjacent
large tree, sufficiently near to shelter it from the ruder
gales, but not close enough to obstruct the light and
air by which it was nourished. Such a tree might have
a series of large and rather uniform rings, during the
period of its protection by its neighbour; and these
might be followed by a series of stinted and irregular
ones, occasioned by the destruction of its protector.
The same storm might have mutilated some trees, and
half-uprooted others: these latter might strive to support themselves for years, making but little addition, by
stinted layers, to the thickness of their stems; and then,
having thrown out new roots, they might regain their
former rate of growth, until a new tempest again
shook them from their places. Similar effects might
result from floods and the action of rivers on the
trees adjacent to their banks. But all these local
and peculiar circumstances would disappear, if a
sufficient number of sections could be procured from

fossil trees, spread over a considerable extent of country.

Similar rings might however furnish other intimations of a successive existence of these trees.

On examining some rings remarkable for their size and position, we might find, for instance, in one section, two remarkably large rings, separated from another large ring, by one very stinted ring, and this followed, after three ordinary years, by two very small and two very large rings. Such a group might be indicated by the letters—

o L L s o o o s L L o o

where o denotes an ordinary year, or ring, L a large one, and s a small or stinted ring.

If such a group occurred in the sections of several different trees, it might fairly be attributed to general causes.

Let us now suppose such a group to be found near the centre of one tree, and towards the external edge or bark of another; we should certainly conclude, that the tree near whose bark it occurred was the more ancient tree; that it had been advanced in age when *that* group of seasons occurred which had left their mark near the pith of the more recent tree, which was young at the time those seasons happened. If,

on counting the rings of this tree, we found that there
were, counting inward from the bark to this remarkable group, three hundred and fifty rings, we should
justly conclude that, three hundred and fifty years
before the death of this tree, which we will call A,
the other, which we will call B, and whose section we
possess, had then been an old tree.　If we now search
towards the centre of the second tree B, for another
remarkable group of rings; and if we also find a similar
group near the bark of a third tree, which we will call
C; and if, on counting the distance of the second
group from the first in B, we find an interval of 420
rings, then we draw the inference that the tree A, 350
years before its destruction, was influenced in its
growth by a succession of ten remarkable seasons,
which also had their effect on a neighbouring tree B,
which was at that time of a considerable age.　We
conclude further, that the tree B was influenced in its
youth, or 420 years before the group of the ten seasons,
by another remarkable succession of seasons, which also
acted on a third tree, C, then old.　Thus we connect
the time of the death of the tree A with the series of
seasons which affected the tree C in its old age, at a
period 770 years antecedent.　If we could discover
other trees having other cycles of seasons, capable of
identification, we might trace back the history of that
ancient forest, and possibly find in it some indications
for conjecturing the time occupied in forming the stratum
in which it is embedded.

The application of these views to ascertaining the age of submerged forests, or to that of peat mosses, may possibly connect them ultimately with the chronology of man. Already we have an instance of a wooden hut with a stone hearth before it, and burnt wood on it, and a gate leading to a pile of wood, discovered at a depth of fifteen feet below the surface of a bog in Ireland : and it was found that this hut had probably been built when the bog had only reached half its present thickness, since there were still fifteen feet of turf below it.

The realization of the views here thrown out will require the united exertions of many individuals patiently exerted through a series of years. The first step must be to study fully the relations of the annual rings in every part of an individual tree. The effect of a favourable or unfavourable season on a section near the root must be compared with the influence of the same circumstance on its growth towards the top of the tree. Vertical sections also must be examined in order to register the annual additions to its height, and to compare them with its increase of thickness. Every branch must be traced to its origin, and its sections be registered. The means of identifying the influence of different seasons in various sections of the same individual tree and its branches being thus attained, the conclusions thus arrived at must be applied to several trees under similar circumstances, and such modifica-

tions must be applied to them as the case may require;
and before any general conclusions can be reached respecting a tract of country once occupied by a forest,
it will be necessary to have a considerable number of
sections of trees scattered over various parts of it.

NOTE N.

ON A METHOD OF MULTIPLYING ILLUSTRATIONS FROM WOOD-CUTS.

FINDING the number of wood-cuts necessary to explain the parts of the Calculating Engine considerable, and the expense great, it appeared to me that the method of copying by casting might, perhaps, be employed for the purpose of diminishing the evil.

The plan which occurred to me was, to make a drawing of that portion of the mechanism required to be explained, which should contain every part necessary for its action, and, in some cases, even the framework requisite for its support. Such a drawing would be far too complicated for the ordinary reader, and might appear confusion even to the contriver of the machine. This drawing was then to be sent to the wood-cutter to be engraved, and on its return, it was to be sent to the stereotype founder, for the purpose of having any number of fac-similes made in type-metal. Now, each of these plates would, like the original wood-cut, express the drawing in *relief*, and, by cutting away any line in the plate, that line would be removed in the impression.

The first thing to be done was, to remove from one of these stereotype plates every line, *except* those which formed the *framing* of the mechanism. The next step was, to remove from another of those plates *all* the framing, and every other line, except those which represented two or three of the principal wheels and levers.

If there should be many such parts, several plates might be taken, on each of which some few parts, not interfering with each other, might be allowed to remain. Other plates might then be taken, on which the parts given on two or more of the former plates, might be allowed to remain, and other plates might again contain combinations of three or more of these. Thus, by a series of plates, commencing with the simplest portions of the mechanism, we might gradually advance through the various combinations, up to the original wood-cut, which, by means of such steps, might be made perfectly intelligible.

The original wood-cut will be more expensive, on account of the additional work contained in it; but its

multiplication by casting is a cheap process; and the
cutting away some of the lines of each plate, and
dotting others, by removing small portions at short
intervals, which might, in different plates, require to be
represented as passing behind other lines, is not a
work of much difficulty or expense. The quantity of
illustrations, all printed with the letter-press, which
this plan admits of, renders it possible to explain much
more complicated machinery than could be accomplished by engraving, unless at an expense which
would effectually preclude its application; whilst the
successive picture of every wheel and lever, exhibited
on separate plates if necessary, as well as of every
one of those binary and other combinations which are
employed, will render the machinery intelligible to
a much larger class of persons than those who usually
study such subjects.

The same principle may be applied to coloured
geological sections and maps. The whole drawing
having been sent to the wood-cutter, as many stereotype fac-similes may be made from his block as there
are colours to be represented. One plate may then be
taken, from which all the parts are to be scraped out
which are not to be coloured brown; another may be
taken from which all parts not to be coloured green;
and so on for all the rest of the colours. The perfect
identity of the plates will render it easy to preserve
what is technically termed *the register*, that is, to

prevent the overlapping of any one colour on any
other.

As the method here suggested is extremely simple
in its means, it is scarcely possible but that it must
have occurred to others; and it may, perhaps—although I am not aware of it—have been employed on
some occasions. I have, however, thought, that in
giving publicity to it, I should be doing a service to
those whose writings require pictorial illustration, and
especially to those who cultivate the sciences of mechanics and geology. Perhaps, also, the same system
might be applied to multiply, at a cheap rate, the
blocks used in colour printing, both upon paper and
on woven fabrics.

On the opposite page, the reader will find an illustration of this art; it is the same plate as that at page
190: it is not very favourable either as to the degree
of difficulty, or as to the question of economy; but it
is the only one that the subject of this volume admitted, and is quite sufficient to explain the principle.

The figure at the bottom of the page, No. 4, is the
impression from a stereotype plate, which is a fac-
simile from the original wood-cut, engraved for the
illustration. No. 3, the next above, is the impression
from another stereotype plate, from which the lines
marked D and F, on No. 4, have been cut away.

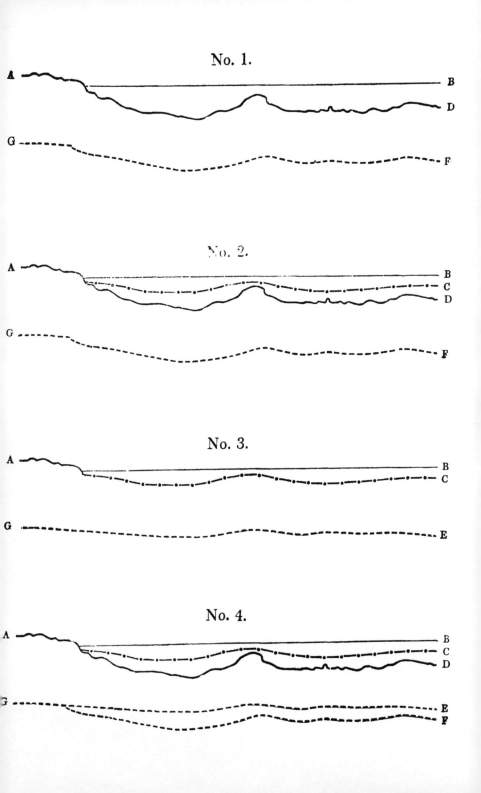

No. 1.

No. 2.

No. 3.

No. 4.

No. 2 is the impression from another plate from which
the line E has been cut away; and No. 1 is an impression from a similar plate, from which the lines C
and E have been cut out.

The four individual plates have been soldered together, and form the stereotype plate of the page referred to.

THE END.

Corrections to Chapter X. and Note E, of the First Edition of the Ninth Bridgewater Treatise.

SOME confusion and error has arisen in the statement of the reasoning by which the refutation of Hume's argument against miracles is supported, although the conclusion itself is perfectly correct. Those who are best acquainted with the extreme difficulty and delicacy of the application of mathematics to the doctrine of chance, will most readily excuse the author for his inattention. It may, however, be useful to point out two of the sources of mistake.

The first results from the different interpretations which may be put on Hume's statement, the second arises from the meaning of the words probability and improbability.

In common language, an event is said to be *probable* when it is more likely to happen than to fail: it is said to be *improbable* when it is more likely to fail than to happen.

Now, an event whose probability is, in mathematical language, $\frac{1}{p}$ will be called probable or improbable, in ordinary language, according as p is less or greater than 2.

If, in mathematical language, $\frac{1}{p}$ expresses the *probability* of an event happening, $1 - \frac{1}{p}$ expresses the probability of its failing, or the *improbability* of its happening.

Another source of error has arisen from not distinguishing between the probability of independent witnesses concurring in a statement before they make it, and the probability of the truth of their testimony after they have given it.

Throughout the inquiry, the term *falsehood* is applied generally to error, whether arising from accident or intention.

THE READER IS REQUESTED TO MAKE THE ALTERATIONS IN THE TEXT WITH A PEN.

Page 120, last line but 3, *read*—" that the fact did not occur."

„ — last line, *read*—" that the fact did not occur."

Page 121, lines 5 and 6, *read*, "would be more probable than that the fact which it endeavours to establish did not occur."

  „ — line 11, *for* " probability" *read* "improbability."

  „ 125, line 7, *for* "true" *read* " false."

  „ 127, and to the end of the Chapter.—It is to be observed that the whole of this reasoning applies only to the inquiry into the chance of the concurrence of independent witnesses previously to their giving their testimony.

The probability, *after they have concurred*, which that concurrence gives to the truth of the event, must be deduced from the following inquiry, which should be substituted for that in the note E, p. 176.

Let us now examine the probability of the truth of an event (whose probability, unsupported by any testimony, is $\frac{1}{q}$) attested to have occurred by the testimony of n independent, uncollusive witnesses, whose probability of falsehood is $\frac{1}{p}$ for each.

There are two views which may be taken of the improbability of miracles. We may suppose an urn to contain balls of only two colours, white and black, from which m balls have been drawn, all black; and the event testified is, that a white ball was the $\overline{m + 1}^{\text{th}}$.

Or we may consider the urn to contain m numbers, and the testimony to assert that a given number i was drawn at the first extraction.

The former of these cases is that which is analogous

to the miracle alluded to in the text. It has been observed that m persons have died without any resurrection, and the probability of the death without resurrection of the $(m+1)^{\text{th}}$ is $\dfrac{m+1}{m+2}$, and the improbability of such an occurrence, independently of testimony, is $\dfrac{1}{m+2}$; which is therefore the probability of a contrary occurrence, or that of a person being raised from the dead.

Now only two hypotheses can be formed, collusion being, by hypothesis, out of the question: either the event did happen, and the witnesses agree in speaking the truth, the probability of their concurrence being $\left(1-\dfrac{1}{p}\right)^n$, and of that of the hypothesis being $\dfrac{1}{m+2}$; or the event did not happen, and the witnesses agree in a falsehood, the probability of their concurrence being $\left(\dfrac{1}{p}\right)^n$, and that of the hypothesis $\dfrac{m+1}{m+2}$.

The probability of the witnesses speaking truth, and the event occurring, is therefore,

$$\frac{\left(1-\frac{1}{p}\right)^n \frac{1}{m+2}}{\left(1-\frac{1}{p}\right)^n \frac{1}{m+2} + \left(\frac{1}{p}\right)^n \frac{m+1}{m+2}} = \frac{(p-1)^n}{(p-1)^n + m + 1};$$

and the probability of their falsehood is,

$$\frac{\left(\frac{1}{p}\right)^n \frac{m+1}{m+2}}{\left(1-\frac{1}{p}\right)^n \frac{1}{m+2} + \left(\frac{1}{p}\right)^n \frac{m+1}{m+2}} = \frac{m+1}{(p-1)^n + m + 1}.$$

But, according to Hume's argument, the falsehood of the witnesses must be more improbable than the occurrence of the miracle. But the probability of the occurrence of the miracle, independent of testimony, is $\dfrac{1}{m+2}$.

Hence, $\dfrac{m+1}{(p-1)^n + m + 1} < \dfrac{1}{m+2}$;

or $(m+1) \cdot (m+2) < (p-1)^n + m + 1$;

$(p-1)^n > (m+1) \cdot (m+2) - (m+1) > (m+1)^2$;

which is true, if

$$n > \dfrac{2 \log. (m+1)}{\log. (p-1)}.$$

It follows, therefore, that however large m may be, or however great the quantity of experience against the occurrence of a miracle, (provided only that there are persons whose statements are more frequently correct than incorrect, and who give their testimony in favour of it without collusion,) a certain number n can ALWAYS be found; so that *it shall be a greater improbability that their unanimous statement shall be a falsehood, than that the miracle shall occur.*

Let us now suppose each witness to state one falsehood for every ten truths, or $p = 11$, and $m = 1000,000,000,000$;

$$\text{then, } n > \dfrac{2 \log. (10^{12} + 1)}{\log. 10} > 24.$$

or twenty-five such witnesses are sufficient.

If the witnesses only state one falsehood for every hundred truths, then thirteen such witnesses are sufficient.